M. A. Bengough

So near akin

Vol. I

M. A. Bengough

So near akin
Vol. I

ISBN/EAN: 9783337040000

Printed in Europe, USA, Canada, Australia, Japan

Cover: Foto ©ninafisch / pixelio.de

More available books at **www.hansebooks.com**

SO NEAR AKIN.

A Novel.

BY

M. A. BENGOUGH.

IN THREE VOLUMES.
VOL. I.

LONDON:
RICHARD BENTLEY AND SON,
Publishers in Ordinary to Her Majesty the Queen.
1891.

(All rights reserved.)

CONTENTS OF VOL. I.

CHAPTER		PAGE
I.	A Disgrace to the Family	1
II.	Her Son's Mother ...	27
III.	Anne's Miracle Play	51
IV.	The Wide, Wide World	77
V.	Cousin and Aunt	108
VI.	The Family Skeleton comes out of the Cupboard ...	134
VII.	The Whirligig of Time	160
VIII.	Brings about its Revenges	185
IX.	After the Conquest	217
X.	"People in Society"	246
XI.	Hester's Convert	269

SO NEAR AKIN.

CHAPTER I.

A DISGRACE TO THE FAMILY.

It was a quite aggressively respectable house. The whole neighbourhood, indeed, was redolent of respectability; for this was Clapham—in the latter end of its palmy days, it is true, but still some time before the era of the Junction or of the Oxford movement. This house in particular, might have been built to order for a serious family; there was a well-to-do comeliness in every line of it, but a comeliness tempered with sobriety. Even now, amidst the dreary dimness of a drizzling autumn twilight, it kept up its dignity. The very flowers in the garden seemed to have been trained, like so many gladiators, to die decently. No trailing stalks or dishevelled heads were here; they died, but they did not surrender. The place was a very epic of respectability.

So it seemed to the man who stood leaning against the gatepost. And a smile grew about his lips as he looked—a smile most like an inaudible chuckle.

"Just like Thomas," he said.

Then he picked up a bundle tied up in a blue check handkerchief, slung it across his stick, and the stick across his shoulder, gave a rapid touch to his hat, imparting the true vagabond cock, and strolled leisurely down the garden path. The little yellow puddles in the gravel soaked in through his ragged boots, water dripped from the brim of his battered hat, two buttons that did not match, and an elaborate system of pins, kept together his frayed and faded blue coat. Altogether he felt effective, and he was so—a figure as entirely out of keeping with his surroundings as his fondest wish could frame.

The shutters were up and the curtains drawn; when the front-door was opened a flood of lamplight and warm air streamed out to meet him, and gave all needful point to the contrast. There was nothing else warm about the welcome; the butler who answered the bell was more than cool.

"Master never gives anything at the door," he said shortly, eyeing the visitor with strong disfavour.

"Is not your master at home?"

"He can't see you."

"I think he will, if you will do me the

kindness to say that Mr. William would like to speak to him for a moment."

The stranger's voice was singularly well modulated; without being harmonious it impressed itself on the hearer, and it had its effect. Perhaps, however, it was not only his voice that moved Mr. Graves into sudden relenting. He did not address Mr. William as "sir," nor did he formally invite him to enter; but he muttered something about letting master know, and stood aside. The family skeleton glided meekly in; the chuckle in his eye could almost be heard as he sat humbly down on the edge of a hall chair.

He sat there for some time. His arrival seemed to have made some sensation. Not upstairs, where Captain Paton was at that moment solemnly dressing for the five o'clock solemnity of dinner. But, from downstairs, the servants suddenly began to come and go. The two maids kept passing across the hall. They did not always remember what they had come to do, but they never forgot what it was they had come to see, and they made the most of their opportunities. Mr. William felt his spirits steadily rising. He knew they guessed something of the situation; from a professional point of view he was fond of playing to a pit audience, and now he began to play to this one. He did not speak; he did not seem to know they were there. But in dumb show, with no other help than genius and a red pocket-handkerchief, he began to give pathetic domestic drama to the maids at one minute, and, at the next, low comedy to the little butler's assistant till he vanished into the dining-room with a clatter of falling spoons and a smothered shout.

At the same moment there was a diversion. The nursery was evidently in revolt. There was a scuffling struggle on the top landing, a subdued remonstrance, a child's shrill rebellious treble. The next moment, sliding down the banisters at break-neck speed, taking the curves in gallant fashion which yet brought Mr. William's heart into his mouth, came a little girl. How she finally alighted, safe and breathless, at his feet he did not know; she was so light there was scarcely the sound of a drop as she swung herself to the floor. Then she leaned for a moment, flushed and panting, against the rail and looked at him.

For his part he could only look at her; he had seldom seen such a vision of childhood. She was nine years old, but did not look her age. Her hair was of that pure gold, like raw silk, which does not often outlast actual infancy. It was kept short, after the fashion of the day, but round the temples it curled of itself into loose, soft rings of irresistible curve. She had the face of one of Sir Joshua's most heavenly-minded cherubs; the limpid candour of her blue eyes would have converted a cynic to belief in virtue. Altogether she was the type of the predestined martyr to good conduct made familiar by a certain class of Sunday-school books. But Anne Paton possessed a magnificent constitution, and enjoyed (not altogether metaphorically) the reputation of being the naughtiest child in the neighbourhood. She was plainly dressed in a grey merino frock. The short sleeves and low neck showed off the perfect childish modelling of her arms and shoulders; round her throat she wore a string of some small, pearly-tinted foreign shells.

The vision spoke, still a little breathless. "She wanted to keep me, but she said it was father's brother downstairs, and so of course you are my uncle, and all little girls go and see their uncles. And if I had not come I might not have seen you at all, because I mayn't go down to dessert for a month because I squirted Henry Stephens and spoiled his clean frill. Are you going to stay to dinner? and are you my uncle Will?"

"Yes; it is, it is your long-lost uncle. And you—you are Nancy Paton."

The child was in his arms at the word.

"Oh! you dear naughty uncle! They said you were naughty, and no good people ever call me that. Oh! I have hoped and hoped some day to be called Nancy. I hate Anne; it sounds so good."

Uncle Will's chuckle exploded softly at last.

"So they told you I was naughty, Nancy? Yet you were not afraid of me."

"You see, I am so naughty myself," said Anne, with simple candour.

"And do you think I look as black as I'm painted?"

The child slipped from his arms and stood back to take a look at him.

"Were you painted? I see you are a little smudged still, but I suppose the rain has washed it off; you don't look black, to speak of, now. But of course I should have known you were not a good man."

"Indeed, and how?"

"Good people are always tidy, and never use pins; when they go out in the rain they take umbrellas. And they don't call me Nancy. Uncle Will," she said abruptly, "can you dance a hornpipe?"

The actor's eyes twinkled. They were curious eyes, small and deepset, of indefinite colour; changeable too in hue, it seemed, like those of the not then immortalized Pied Piper. "I have done so, on occasion," he said. "You know, or perhaps you don't, that your grandfather was a sailor."

"Yes, that was why I asked. And will you then? Oh, will you?"

She was clinging round his knees, suddenly she pulled him down to listen; even Anne dared not name the bribe aloud.

"If you will I—I'll whistle for you," she whispered.

When Captain Paton, in the full glory of evening costume, opened the door of his dressing-room, he caught, first, the sound of a clear bird-like whistle, unmistakably Anne's, trilling out a nautical air. With this was mingled a peculiar sound of alternate thump and double-shuffle, varied by an occasional finger snap. And when he came out on to the landing, too much bewildered as yet even for horror, the first thing he saw was his daughter, perched lightly on the rounded end of the stair-rail, whistling ecstatically as she watched a draggled-looking individual performing a rollicking hornpipe in the middle of the hall.

"Anne!"

The whistling broke short off, like the song of a startled bird; she slipped from her perch and stood with drooping head and downcast eyes. The dancer, too, came to a stop, and faced round to see what had happened. Then Captain Paton recognized him. He had not done so at first. Prepared though he was for his visitor, he had not expected anything so bad as this; now it flashed upon him that this disreputable yet jovial vagabond was really his brother Will. He had been prepared for shabbiness, for misery and degradation, even for abject poverty and distress, for anything and everything but this. In the shock of that recognition Anne was forgotten; he took no further notice of her as she lingered on the stairs, uncertain whether it would be better policy to go or stay. She thought he was too angry to speak, but in truth the child had faded from his mind. The memory of older, earlier ties, strained to snapping long ago, came between him and all the present, except that one ragged, wet, draggled irrepressible, who advanced to meet him at the foot of the stairs. Captain Paton had not an expressive face, scarcely more so than one of his own figure-heads. But on this occasion it was possible to gather something of his mind from his countenance. It was nothing flattering.

"My brother!" exclaimed Mr. William,

in thrilling tones. He seemed about to clasp him, as he had done Anne, in a damp embrace. But suddenly he turned away his head, and retreated a step or two, extending towards the Captain an averting, deprecating hand.

"Forgive me," he murmured, "I had forgotten—what I am, what you are. I thought for a moment of what we both were years ago, in our father's cottage, at our mother's knee. 'Twas natural, but 'twas unfitting. Your pardon, Thomas."

He had turned his head again. From that mobile countenance every trace of levity had disappeared ; his very eyes looked more hollow and sunken.

For a moment his brother stared at him with a wooden bewilderment. Then he gave up all attempts to follow suit to such a conversational lead as that, and started afresh on his own account.

"This is not the place for an interview, William," he said. "And I must say that I am grieved and pained—seriously distressed, that you should have compromised the character of my establishment, corrupted, I may say, the morals of my domestics, encouraged the deplorable instincts I have to lament in my child——"

"It was I, sir, who begged my uncle William to dance, and who offered to whistle for him. I'm very sorry, father, I forgot," said poor Anne.

"Go, child, and reflect on your conduct. I do not wish to see you again until I send for you. You are a great grief to me, Anne."

The reaction, the excitement of all the circumstances, broke the child down. She burst into sobs more angry than penitent.

"Then I wish you would give your horrid wicked daughter right away to your naughty brother to be his little Nancy! I'm not a grief to him. And they might put me into a story book, with the bad end I'm sure to come to, and you could give it to Hester, and she and Henry Stephens might read it together. I wouldn't mind about the bad end, if I might have all the good time first. And I'm not a grief to you, Uncle Will, am I?"

She clung to him in her sudden passion of revolt.

"Upon my word," he said, with a lapse into his natural, unhistrionic manner, "I don't think that's a bad notion the child has got. Come, Thomas, exchange is no robbery, you know; suppose we make an exchange—your daughter for my son."

"Your son?"

"To be sure; didn't you remember that? Affectionate brother! Yes, you are quite right, you *did* forget to inquire after Mrs.

William. Theresa is quite well, thank you; stouter than she used to be, but a fine figure for maternal tragedy still. If George could but play up to her—but he is a stick, a mere stick. 'Pon my soul, Thomas, I think we had better exchange."

"Is that his name? My cousin George! Is he like you? How old is he? Why didn't you bring him?"

In the new excitement Anne forgot the depths of her disgrace.

"I didn't bring him because he wouldn't come. He is sixteen years old, and is my exact antipodes in every respect. Think of it, Thomas; I assure you it is worth thinking of. Going—an amiable youth who would be a credit to any well-ordered establishment, who would like nothing better than to join, or cut out, Master Henry Stephens with your younger daughter, in those charming Sabbath hours of literary recreation to which——"

"Forbear this ribaldry, William, at least in the presence of my child. Master Henry Stephens is one whom any parent might gladly see his son copy, and next heir to a baronetcy. And *my* family do not read profane literature on the Sabbath."

"There's your naughty uncle put his cloven foot into it again, Nancy!" ejaculated the unabashed actor in a stage aside.

There was a pause. Then Captain Paton resumed—

"If by your extraordinary proposal you mean to imply that you even now repent of bringing up your unhappy son to follow the degrading career on which you yourself are embarked—I will consult Mrs. Paton, and I have no doubt that arrangements might be made. Of course, I could not admit him into my family circle without some probationary period, passed among reputable surroundings. But I cannot forget that the youth is my brother's son, and that that brother can still wish to save his child."

Will Paton shook a doubtful head; the twinkle rose again in his eye.

"Your words, Thomas, recall me, as ever, to myself," he said seriously. "You are truly kind, as usual, but I see now it can never be. You will not reckon without Jane" (Captain Paton winced at the familiarity); "I had all but reckoned without Theresa. And Theresa would never part from the boy. He is as little like her as he is like me, except in looks; but she thinks him perfection in himself, and a saving clause as regards us. It is as good as a play, sir, to see those two together. So, as I suppose you will scarcely give me your Nancy here—good-bye, Nancy; good-bye, brother Thomas; give my love to Jane and kiss Hester for me. The eternal wanderer passes from innocence and domestic bliss, and from the home that ne'er may smile for him, curse-driven forth into the stormy night—*en route* for Brighton, where the company is due on Wednesday next, to have the honour of performing, before the first gentleman in Europe, the pleasing comedy of 'Paul Pry,' title-rôle by Mr. W. Paton."

He shouldered his bundle once more, jammed his battered hat firmly on his head, passed his expressive hand across his eyes, and prepared to sally forth. Stiffer than ever, in a truly British awkwardness of giving, Captain Paton stopped him at the very door.

"I have many claims upon me," he said, in an attempt at a hurried whisper; "but if you are going out to—to—homelessness and starvation——"

There was a certain crisp rustle, far less unfamiliar to the actor's ears than his brother supposed. He recoiled this time with an unaffected start.

"Bless your thick head and your kind heart, Tom," he exclaimed, in unconventionally clear tones. "It always was a shame to green you; it is too disgracefully easy. I can't take your money, my boy. Don't you understand? I'm no worse off than you are."

"Your coat, your hat!" He could say no more.

"All properties, nothing else; borrowed to get a rise out of you, Tom. Don't bear malice, old chap; I am immensely grateful, so is Theresa, so is George; but homeless, destitute—ha! ha! ha! excuse me; ten thousand pardons, but—ha! ha! ha!"

It was not in human nature not to slam

the door then. Captain Paton did slam it, hearing even through the closing crash the inexpressibly hilarious laughter dying in gusts along the garden path. It would scarcely have soothed his feelings to have seen his brother lying back in the hackney-coach which awaited him just round the corner, wiping the mirth-born moisture from his eyes again and again, as he rehearsed the whole interview as it would appear to his appreciative wife.

Captain Paton could not trust himself to speak, and in fact anger never made him eloquent. With a gesture of dismissal which his brother might have envied, he waved Anne from him, and himself turned into the parlour and took up the newspaper; but he did not read. His wife looked up, at his entrance, from the netting of a chronic green silk purse; she read the storm-signal on his brow, and began to think what there was for dinner. She was a timid-looking, willowy creature, like a faint steel-engraving from the Ladies' Keepsake, blonde to aggravation, and dressed to intensify it. The orphan heiress of an old merchant family, it was she who had brought to her husband wealth and social consideration; but never was gift less presumed upon by the giver. It is doubtful whether she had ever realized that he was in her debt.

Meanwhile Anne, still struggling with the stormy sobs of a child's sense of hopeless naughtiness and disgrace, climbed slowly up the stairs to the nursery. A pretty little brown-haired girl was sitting demurely on a low stool at the extreme edge of the hearthrug, her little bronze-slippered toes kept religiously on the virtuous side of forbidden ground, her little mittened hands folded on her lap.

She was dressed for dessert and might not disarrange herself: an engaging little figure in her white frock, with broad yellow sash and amber beads. But beside Anne her brown and rosy, dove-eyed prettiness faded into insignificance. Hester was not formed for comparisons.

The sisters were on fair terms, but on fair terms only. Anne had a considerable contempt for Hester; Hester could scarcely help feeling morally superior to Anne.

"Oh! sister," she began, "was father very much displeased?"

Anne choked down a sob in a silent toss of defiance.

"Dear Anne, I wish you were not always getting into trouble."

"Well, I'm not going to get into much more. I'm going to live with Uncle Will and have Cousin George for a brother.

I've had enough of sisters; the stupidest boy—even Henry Stephens—is more amusing than a girl."

" Do you think Henry is a stupid boy? I think he is nice; and he is very good."

"Ah! you may say that, Miss Hester," put in the nurse, in a tone that foreboded a moral.

" Is he good, nurse?" asked Anne, with sudden interest.

" If *you* don't know it, Miss Anne, I don't know who should; after what he has to put up with from you."

"Well; but very, very good?"

" Yes."

" I am glad," said Anne. "Really good enough to die like the boys in books?"

"And if he does, you very wicked girl, I wonder where do you expect to go to? And he consumptive, like his poor dear pa!"

"Oh! if he did, would it be murder?" said Hester, her soft eyes growing round with terror.

"Of course not, silly," retorted Anne, with more assurance than she felt. "Besides, he isn't going to; I know he isn't really good enough for that. He hasn't forgiven me yet, and the boys in books do that when they are dying—send for the wicked boy that killed them to forgive him. Henry hasn't sent for me."

"Oh! Anne, I'm sure he has forgiven you."

"I don't care; he won't for the next time."

"What do you mean?"

"Ah!"

"What are you going to do?"

But neither threats nor entreaties could extort from Anne anything but peals of impish laughter. Finally Hester had to depart unsatisfied. As soon as she was gone Anne flung herself on the floor in a passion of tears and sobs. She did not greatly value the privilege of dessert when she had it; but she felt bitterly the sense of outlawry implied in its withdrawal, and all the fierceness of her wrath centred upon Henry Stephens.

CHAPTER II.

HER SON'S MOTHER.

IN the wisdom of the East there is a custom by which a man, upon becoming the proud and happy parent of a son and heir, merges his own identity in that of his son, and from being known as Ali or Yussuf becomes the Father-of-Adhem or Selim as the case may be. Mrs. Stephens, then, was known primarily, even to herself, as the mother of the future Sir Henry. Like the nimbus seen floating above the cradles of certain future saints, the glory of the coming title played around the head of Mrs. Stephens' first-born, and its lustre was reflected more faintly upon her. She, reverential by nature and doting by maternity, scarcely realized her own share in this glory: if it is possible to conceive of an apologetic necessity, Mrs. Stephens was that metaphysical phenomenon. Even the heir to a baronetcy is under the vulgar obligation of having a mother, but towards him she so conducted herself as to render his commonplace entrance into the world as little galling to him, and as little obtrusive to the generality as might be. To all her numerous family she was a devoted, an absorbingly devoted mother; but for Henry, even at the early age of thirteen, her devotion was tempered with respect.

The prestige was his alone; he had no rival to dread even in her memory. Upon the late Mr. Stephens this light had not risen; he had never been the future Sir Joseph. A series of family catastrophes, in the first year after his death, had left the youthful Henry unexpectedly heir apparent. Even had it been otherwise it would have detracted little from the splendour of his position. Joseph Stephens had not been the man to make an impression under any circumstances. He had been; he was not: to the general public his biography was comprised in those words. To him might have been applied the epitaph of a Prince of Wales—

> "Since it is only Fred,
> Who was alive and is dead,
> Why, there's no more to be said!"

The very disease which had shuffled him gently and considerately off this mortal coil owed its name to the doctors, who did not choose to confess themselves unable to assign it any local habitation. As a matter of fact, it had been as vague as the rest of him; as he had dropped through life so he finally dropped out of it, with no more tangible reason for the last step than for any of the preceding ones.

Mrs. Stephens was left a widow, indifferently provided for, except with children, and with that splendour which had not yet dawned upon her horizon. She wept and gathered her children round her—solemn five-year-old Henry, John, Mary, Joseph, and James—all of them, down to the two-months-old twins; and looking on them she was comforted. Henry requested his dear mamma's permission to repeat a hymn; John and Mary made such cruelly practical remarks about the pit-hole and poor dear papa as only unimaginative children of three and four can do. The twins thrust aimless fists into her eyes and clawed at her cap as they lay in her arms on the sofa; and she could not feel her life to be a blank, felt it even less than she would have wished. Free from all other ties she now first found her true vocation. She had been an ordinarily good wife, but first and foremost and above all things she was born to be a mother, and to motherhood she henceforth devoted herself. So soon as the financial situation was made clear to her she rose to the situation. She worked harder and with less sleep than any two servants, and seemed to thrive upon it. She was by turns cook, housemaid, tailor and dressmaker, besides being nurse always; she had even handled the mangle and the blacking-brush. Yet she kept up with society and never degenerated into a household drudge.

This seems to be the description of a clever, superior woman; but intellectually Mrs. Stephens was rather silly, and had no pretensions to being superior. It is true that she had come to Clapham encompassed by traditions of some uncommon degree of education, but no one knew exactly the origin of the idea. It had soon faded and died. By the end of her first year of married life Maria Stephens' conversation was considered below par even by the not dazzlingly intellectual society of Clapham. After the birth of her first child she scarcely opened a book, except the volume of sermons she went to sleep over on Sundays. Her mind did not become a blank, far from it; she had a well-stored and an active one. Only, one by one, the more abstruse contents of her mental library were consigned to the lobby of oblivion to make room for whole encyclopedias of nursery and domestic lore and endless files of Clapham chronicle.

This last possession no doubt helped to make her what she was, a generally popular woman. Not generally adored or respected, indeed pretty generally laughed at, but every one was her well-wisher. It has been said she was not generally adored, yet she had her devotees. The rector of the parish called her the Cornelia of Clapham. Perhaps his appreciation was not quite disinterested ; it increased perceptibly in keenness and fervour during the holidays ; he was an elderly widower with three big sons in the hobbledehoy stage of objectionability, and it was thought Cornelia might have added these jewels to her own at any time within the last eight years, had she so pleased. In a strictly platonic and irreproachable fashion Captain Paton was another of her admirers. He never wearied of expressing his admiration ; her virtues formed the text of so many domestic lectures that Mrs. Paton might have had as much reason for hating the very sound of her name as Anne had for disliking Henry's. Yet Mrs. Paton bore no malice; in a languid and colourless way she was good friends with her exemplar. They called each other Jane and Maria and kissed at meeting, Maria smartly and solidly, Jane dissolving as it were into a sort of diluted caress. They were next-door neighbours, their children had been playmates from their cradles, they each found servants for the other, and employed the same tradespeople. Mrs. Paton lent Mrs. Stephens patterns of her children's more fashionable clothes, and Mrs. Stephens reciprocated with recipes for jam or home-made wine and dodges in domestic economy. Separately and together the two families were an edification to the parish. For eight years they had stood the test of the closest neighbourhood and stood it well. One reason might be that, with all their familiarity, their intercourse kept clear of the danger of unceremoniousness. Nothing with which Captain Paton had to do could possibly be other than ceremonious.

When any friend of the family wished to make himself particularly agreeable, he would turn from watching the innocent sports of Henry and Anne, to remark with a smile what a charming pair they made. So far as looks went, no doubt they did. Not that Henry's good looks were in the same style as Anne's; where she was piquant he was correct; he was no vision, unless the British aristocrat can be called a vision. Patrician, conventionally, spectacularly patrician, was what he looked to the backbone—especially, perhaps, in the backbone. Mrs. Paton, who was poetical but unfortunately hazy as to contexts in her quotations, had often murmured that dear Henry was so clearly one of Nature's noblemen. She meant no sarcasm, yet she perpetrated a pretty sharp one. For every one knew that Henry's aristocratic appearance was the result of one of those freaks by which nature does set believers in heredity at defiance. Mrs. Stephens' ancestry was respectable, but far indeed from being distinguished; nor had the race of country squires, from whom he traced his descent on the other side, been of a kind likely to transmit any superlative degree of refinement to their posterity. The title itself, though supported by a suitable though not magnificent amount of landed property, was of late creation and had no very exalted account to give of its origin. Every one knew this, but it was tacitly ignored, and nature favoured such ignoring.

All the little Stephenses had more or less of this unaccountable air of birth about them. They were a family for any mother to be proud of, and they were not thrown away upon this one. The time to see them in their glory was at half-past ten on Sunday mornings, when at the first sound of the bell the whole train came two and two, hand in hand, down the garden path, to join forces with the Patons at the gate. First, John with Mary soberly cheerful and elder-sisterly. Then Joseph and James, comely and unindividualized, as inseparable as the real twins Susan and Sarah, now just eight years old, but kept babies so long that Anne looked down on them from immeasurable heights, and even Hester, though no older than they, felt almost motherly towards them. The rear would be brought up by Mrs. Stephens leaning on Henry's arm, he carrying her reticule and a large white shawl with a brilliant border; on threatening days the family umbrella was substituted for the shawl.

The day after William Paton's visit was decidedly an umbrella Sunday, chilly with fog and gloomy with the foreshadowings of November. Henry was absent from the procession; his defection was attributed to the results of Anne's hydropathic treatment at the beginning of the week, and she was condemned to walk behind in solitary disgrace. Unwisely condemned, as she improved the opportunity and relieved her feelings by stepping lovingly and carefully into every puddle she could find on the way, with satisfaction only tempered by the fact that she dared not make any splash.

The walk to church was a dull and rather long one, and Anne had an active mind which she gladly exercised on the affairs of her elders and betters. It is probable, however, that only the delights of hearing what was not intended for her kept up her attention. Yet older people might well have found something intrinsically funny in the conversation of three people whose styles were at once definite and antagonistic. Mrs. Paton's, indeed, was not aggressive, but her remarks were usually altogether unconnected with the subject in hand, and dropped isolated across the war of tongues like faint-hearted minute-guns that scarcely expect a reply. But with Captain Paton and Mrs. Stephens Greek met Greek. His style, especially on Sunday, was exhortatory, hers was meandering, but neither yielded to the other in fluency, and neither was above taking the meanest advantage in seizing an opening.

Mrs. Paton hoped dear Henry was not seriously indisposed. Captain Paton saw an opportunity of improving the occasion to Anne, but Mrs. Stephens was aware of it too, and got first start on her own subject.

"I hope not, my love; no, I think I should not say seriously. I was very anxious about him on Friday evening; in fact, I am quite stiff this morning still. He looked so flushed and feverish, I wanted to send for Dr. Barclay; but he was so disagreeable last time I sent for him at night, and of course we are all poor frail mortals, but I do think that temper is extra sinful in a doctor who, one may say, is conversing daily with death. And if you will take my advice, Jane, and send for Dr. Lamb next time, you will find the difference of being attended by a true Christian."

"Ah! if only doctors would realize as you do the nature of their calling, dear Mrs. Stephens, what a blessed change we should see in the character of the profession. But, alas! so true it is, as that very gracious young man, Mr. Jefferys, was telling us only last Sunday——"

"Mary, my love, Sally's shoe-string has come untied. Put her little foot up on that step and bring her after us; we will go slowly and you can catch us up."

"Yes, we will run and catch you up," said Sarah, with infantine deliberation of utterance.

"No, dear Sally, we will walk fast, but we must not run on the Sabbath."

Mary's mother lost the joy of edification which this remark was calculated to afford her, as she was already off at score with the conversation in her own hands again. Anne heard it, and lingered to show her appreciation by a grimace more hideous than it would have seemed possible for so fair a face to produce. When she next gave ear to the conversation Mrs. Stephens was still in possession of the field.

"And as I said to her: 'Of course, Mary Anne, when I engaged you I could not say, to a pint, how much water you would have to carry up every day; you can see for yourself that Master Henry is very unwell'; (and really he was coughing a regular churchyard cough, as people say, at that very minute, and there *is* nothing like putting the feet in mustard and hot water, as I daresay you know, Captain). I said to her that sickness was a dispensation that might happen in any family, and no notice given bèforehand. But she was so much put out, that sooner than have her in the sulks for a week, and next day Saturday and all, I said I would carry it up myself if she would sit with the twins‘ while they went to sleep; and I think I strained myself a little with using the big can. You see I was in a hurry to get back, for really that girl can scarcely be trusted with the children. I hope Eliza continues to give satisfaction, Jane."

"Except for her hair," murmured Mrs. Paton. "But of course these are matters which are not in our own hands."

"True, Jane," interposed her overjoyed husband; "most providentially true. How far different might have been your lot and mine, the lot of any one of us, had the choice been left to our misguided selves. How often do we see the self-chosen path, fair and smiling at the outset, slope swiftly down to misery and degradation. Yes, we know, Mrs. Stephens, the blessings of a choiceless career. And how few need choose! In the days of our youth, fond and careful parents settle our course of action."

"Didn't you say, Thomas, that Mrs. William Paton's little boy's hair promised to be bright red?"

"There," said the captain courageously, "is a case in point. This, Mrs. Stephens, is a case which has come under my personal observation. Two boys, the children of poor but honest parents, were just entering upon life; that all important moment had come in which their future career was to be determined. The father, a—a—in short a sea-faring man, had destined both for his own profession. The choice was not congenial to the tastes of either youth; the profits and the prospects were small, the hardships many."

"Yes, that's what poor Uncle Ben always used to say. 'More kicks than halfpence.' Poor old man! when he was quite worn out they put him in a coast-guard station on the Lincolnshire coast; it was a great place for Dutch smugglers, but he caught cold and died the first winter of it."

"He died, madam, in the discharge of his duty; what better fate could he desire? Had the youth of whom I was speaking done the same, how far nobler and better in every way might his life have been. But he refused. Regardless of a father's commands, a mother's tears, he chose his own career among the miserable votaries of the stage. His brother, who started in life bare-footed and with one change of clothing done up in a handkerchief, now, under Providence, a comfortable householder, saw him yesterday and scarcely recognized him. I, dear friend, was that poor sailor boy; the strolling player, alas! was my only brother."

"I wonder how much he does get a week," said Mrs. Paton reflectively. "I know nothing about the way such people live."

"I trust not, Jane; I sincerely trust

not. My most earnest hope for any one connected with me would be that such ignorance should be theirs for ever."

"His wife didn't bring him anything. Wasn't it shocking, Maria? He married her out of a strolling company on one of their tours; nobody knows even whether she ever had a father or mother."

"Shocking indeed; I know nothing more unpleasant in a family than any mystery about antecedents. There was that strange story about Sir Archibald Maxwell's second wife; I was quite a girl at the time, but I well remember the impresssion it made upon me. You know——"

The conversation took another turn, but Anne listened no more. Her imagination wandered off along paths dim but somewhat awful. She knew next to nothing of fairy-tales; she had never been allowed to read, nor supposed to hear any, Captain Paton being of opinion that such reading was detrimental to a strict regard for truth. She had few of the properties and dramatis personæ which are ready to the imagination of most children. But to a great extent she had supplied the want by vague creations of her own. Every hint gathered surreptitiously was a seed in fertile soil. Like a child-nation, so this individual child, thrown back upon her own resources, developed myths of her own. Even to a sympathetic listener she could have given no clear account of them; but they were very real to her all the same.

Now, this really incomprehensible discourse took its own legendary form in her mind. The red-haired cousin, the aunt who had never had parents, presented ideas fraught with a weird mystery. There was something goblin-like in the red hair, but it was nothing in comparison to the other suggestion. If Uncle Will had taken her at her word she might now have been familiar with those beings whom he called wife and child. She was almost glad for a moment that she could not go; would they have been gracious to her? Uncle Will had spoken of them with affection. She took the wonder with her into church; it occupied her sufficiently in the long hours of seclusion and propriety in the family pew,—hours through which she seldom got with credit. It was a square pew, and she sat with her back to the pulpit, facing the musicians' gallery at the west end. There was a red-haired bassoon up there; he had a black patch over one eye, and a green glitter in the other; he wore a faded bottle-green coat, and a flame-coloured waistcoat, besprinkled with green roses; and when he applied the brazen serpent-coils to his mouth, and his face reddened and blazed under his exertions, he was a very awe-inspiring and inflammatory spectacle. Anne did not exactly fear him, but she cherished for him a sort of superstitious veneration, as for a being not quite human, whose nature might require propitiation rather than affection. Was the cousin anything like that? The idea was not pleasing; but it was not its absence of romance, its vulgarity, that made it unpleasant to Anne. Commonplace, if cantankerous, John Watson was not commonplace to her.

But neither awe nor mystery in his belongings could affect her feelings towards Uncle Will himself; to him, in one short half hour, the child had fairly lost her heart. He was certainly a queer object, either for warm affection or hero-worship, this Uncle Will. An unromantic ne'er-do-weel, without so much as the tragedy of failure to lend him pathos, at least, if not dignity; a man who really deserved no better character than he was generally credited with; who was considered something of a black sheep even among his own none too scrupulous associates; too much of a buffoon to be a villain, but not too much to be a scamp.

The still future years, as they slowly revealed her horoscope, were to point clearly enough to the red star of revolt as that which had presided over poor Anne's birth. But surely she began to dree her weird early, when she found her first ideal in William Paton.

CHAPTER III.

ANNE'S MIRACLE PLAY.

ON that same Sunday afternoon, Henry Stephens was enjoying all the invalid privileges which a fairly severe cold and cough could extort from an anxious and adoring mamma. A small, but cheerful fire glowed pleasantly in the grate, behind the towering fender; the rather austere horse-hair couch, brought up from the dining-room for his especial benefit, was decked with pillows; beside it, on a little round table, stood a jug of the amber-clear toast and water for which Mrs. Stephens was famous, and a blue and white plate full of oranges in sections. A bound volume of the *Youth's Magazine* lay on the couch from which Henry had just risen. It was his Sunday literature, but perhaps it had begun to pall after some hours almost consecutive reading; at any rate even the well regulated Henry seemed to have had enough of it. He walked, with becoming languor to the window, and decorously smothered a yawn.

Henry was seldom bored; to be so would have been against his principles. He had learned from Mr. Andrews, of "Eyes and No Eyes," that no thoughtful, right-minded boy ought ever to know a dull or uninterested moment. But perhaps a *régime* of sofa and oranges had slightly demoralized him; this afternoon, at any rate, he did feel dull.

It is an instinct with the dull to look out of the window, but in this case Henry could have expected no distractions. The window looked on nothing livelier than a small flagged yard, backed by a high wall overgrown with ivy; the points of the leaves were grey with fog-drops, which splashed monotonously into a puddle among the worn stones. The drippings into a water butt, just below the window, joined the cheerful chorus; the sky was grey, and the flags were brown, and a shabby sparrow, hopping about the yard, would have harmonized with its surroundings if it were ever at all possible for a sparrow to be harmonious. There was a side door in the yard for the use of tradesmen, and beyond was a garden and more ivied wall bounding the Patons' garden next door. Certainly entertainment was the last thing that could be expected from such an outlook.

Henry looked, and yawned again more

frankly. He counted the splashes made by the falling mist-drops, which would not keep time with the measured tick of an aggressive clock. No other sounds broke the stillness; even the fire had subsided into red glow and did not crackle. All at once the handle of the side door rattled in an evidently unpractised hand; then the door creaked upon its hinges—and, enter Anne.

She did not proceed to the back door of the house; with unerring aim she sent a small shower of pebbles pelting against the nursery window — still so-called — before she had noticed that the attention of the occupant was sufficiently attracted already. Certainly her appearance challenged attention. She was bare-headed and in indoor dress, and bore the look defined by nurses as being the result of coming through a quickset hedge, for she was dishevelled, draggled, and awry. As soon as she caught sight of Henry's bewildered face, she called to him in tones piercing with a sort of sweet shrillness.

"Come down and let me in."

"Go to the back door," replied Henry, supplementing his muffled tones with pantomime.

Anne shook her head impatiently.

"There's nobody in," she screamed.

Henry nodded an emphatic contradiction as he croaked out,

"Mary Ann."

"I tell you there isn't. I saw Mary Ann go out with the butcher's boy, ever so long ago," retorted Anne, conveying the information to any one within a quarter of a mile round. "Don't be silly; I'm coming to amuse you, you know you want me, and if you didn't, I should come all the same, because you are sick, you know, and we ought to visit the sick. But you do."

It was true; till that moment Henry had not realized how dull he was.

"Make haste!" cried Anne, stamping imperiously.

Henry hesitated, wavered—and fell. Three minutes later Anne was established in the nursery.

"Now, aren't you glad to see me?" she began.

"You ought not to be here," said Henry, conscience gaining the upper hand so soon as his guilt was an accomplished fact.

"Then you oughtn't to have let me in," retorted his unscrupulous visitor. "Oh, Henry, I should never have expected this of you." She broke into one of her peculiarly mocking peals of laughter as she watched his vain efforts to find a crushing reply. "Never mind that now;

it will keep till they come back from church. Now let us amuse ourselves. You will never guess how much I ought not to be here."

"Indeed, dear Anne, if your own conscience tells you the same thing, let me entreat you to return while it is yet time."

"I will—if I remember it, but I expect I shall put it off till too late. Won't they stare when they find me gone out of a locked room? Hester will think Bogy has really come for me this time."

"A locked room?"

"Yes. Look here." She showed what had been a dainty little sandalled shoe with a yawning rent down one side. "That was done by a nail I didn't see among the ivy. I got down by the ivy through the window. They locked me up because I had spoiled my pelisse and my clean stockings walking in the puddles this morning. Father said I was incorrigible; he said he must still do his duty by me, but it was without hope. Don't look at me like that, Henry. I hate you and everybody. I wish everybody was dead!"

The boy, slow of comprehension by nature, and made duller still by his carefully cherished priggishness, was utterly taken aback when Anne flung herself on her knees by the sofa and her excitement broke down into a storm of despairing sobs. The boy's natural horror and dread of tears, which prompted him to flight, was combated by the prig's desire to improve the occasion. He took refuge in a prolonged fit of coughing. When he had made himself breathless, he thought seriously enough of his condition to feel bound to offer advice.

" Dear Anne," he said, half rising from

the pillows on which he had sunk; "I wish you would listen to me this once; it may be the last time. I sometimes fancy I may not be here long——"

"You'll be here a great deal longer than I shall, if you talk like that," said Anne, angrily, but checking her sobs. "If you don't make yourself pleasant I shall go. I know what you were going to say. But it's just no use at all my trying to be good; I wasn't made the right shape, so I shan't trouble any more. They had much better have given me right away to——"

She stopped short. The next instant her volatile spirits broke out into laughter again.

"Oh, Henry, you should have seen Tompkins' boy just now. He had such a dahlia in his button-hole—one of those very red ones, you know, that grow in the middle walk just at the beginning of the strawberry bed. Does your mamma count those dahlias every morning, like Mr. Fairchild used to count the apples on his favourite tree?"

"My mamma says that Mr. Tompkins is a very serious person, and I am sure he would bring up his household well."

"Who said he didn't? Well, I was watching for Mary Anne to come out—because she always does when he is about—and so by-and-bye she opened the door, and when she saw him she gave such a jump! Like this."

She coyly opened the nursery door and perpetrated a leap and yell that would have done credit to a Red Indian on the war-path.

"Oh, Anne, remember what day it is."

"I do remember. So then Tompkins' boy was afraid she was going to fall down,

I suppose," continued the terrible child, "so he caught her so." She encircled the taper waist of a high-backed chair with one arm; the rest of the description was run through in a rapid pantomime, culminating in a sound slap on the unoffending chair, which presumably changed rôles for the crisis. The immediate result was to knock it over with a crash; certainly the room had not been depressingly quiet since Anne had been in it.

Henry, who had listened more from want of a chance to interrupt than from any interest he took in the subject, gave a deprecatory shudder, and again said:—

"Dear Anne!"

"What's the matter? You can't have a headache; you aren't old enough. Only grown-up people have headaches."

Henry was certainly young enough to resent the implied slight to his age; it made him a little stiffer and more moral in the tone of his reply.

"I have not a headache, but you are heard everywhere, and your tongue runs away with you. Little girls should be seen, and not heard."

"I suppose nobody thought it worth while to say that about little boys; they're too stupid to know how to talk. Oh, how glad I am that I'm not a boy!" said Anne, with more fervour than truth. "What have you been doing to amuse yourself all day?"

"It is not a day for amusing one's self. I have been reading this very interesting and, I trust, improving book. Pray, Anne, since you are here, let us turn this visit to some good account. Let me read you an anecdote out of this."

Anne's face was not encouraging.

"You read like a sermon," she said; "and I hate stories with morals, anyway."

"That is because you are too young to know what is really useful and good," said Henry, not sorry for a chance of retorting the slight on his age, which still rankled.

"Oh, am I, Mr. Old Daddy Longlegs?" exclaimed Anne, nettled in her turn. Then, suddenly changing her mind, "No, don't let us quarrel. I tell you I came to amuse you because you are sick. If you really like that sort of thing"— taking up the volume contemptuously— "I'll read you some. Where is something amusing? Oh, this will do."

For her age she was quick at reading, and still quicker of perception, so she soon mastered the drift of the article in question.

"Oh, this is nice. Listen; this is all about a good little boy that was bitten by a mad dog, and died. He was a dear little boy, just like you, only he was younger. His name was Frederick T. Why do all the people in this book have such funny names? Did you ever know anybody called T.?

"That is not the whole of his name," said Henry, mollified at once by the appeal and by the idea that Anne had suffered a temporary lapse into virtue and propriety. "That is only the first, or, to use the correct word, the initial letter. It would grieve his poor parents, you see, dear Anne, to have their names promulgated in a public magazine, though, being good and magnanimous persons, they would not withhold a narrative so likely to conduce to edification."

He felt much better after that; the more long words Henry could get into a sentence the better he did feel.

"Oh," said Anne. She had been rapidly reviewing the details of the case in hand,

and had not listened; but this was beyond Henry's powers of imagination, so that it was in a tone of the most benign condescension that he continued:—

"Well, dear Anne, I hope you will tell me some more."

"Oh, yes," she said, waking up. "It was his father's pet dog, and he was playing with it, and—— Suppose we play at it. You shall be the little boy, and when it comes to the dying part you shall try how right you can do the good talking, you know, and I'll see how much it is like the real Frederick in the book."

Anything that promised an opening for discourse was a sore temptation to Henry; and, after all, why should it not be improving, a chance for a word in season? Still he demurred.

"But we haven't got a dog."

"Oh, I'll be the dog, I don't mind," said

Anne, magnanimously, and proceeded to show two rows of very capable-looking pearls.

"I think we had better begin further on," said Henry, hastily.

"Very well. One day at breakfast his mamma noticed he couldn't drink his tea. I'm your mamma now."

She seized the jug of toast-and-water, and held it to his lips. Henry was not blessed with a strong imagination; he was thirsty, too, and fond of toast-and-water. At this point, therefore, he forgot his part, and was proceeding to apply the draught to its natural use. But Anne was too quick for him.

"No, stop; you mustn't drink it—you can't, you know. Now, I shall encourage you. What was it, lovey? Wasn't the tea nice?" She experimented in a prolonged sip. "Oh, yes, it is very good. Look at mamma, dear; see how she drinks it."

And Henry saw.

Now toast-and-water does not approve itself to the average adult mind as being exactly nectar fit for the gods, not even such toast-and-water as Mrs. Stephens's, in which the soothing honey and the stimulating lemon gave some sort of flavour to the beverage. But when one is very young, and when it is always represented to one in the light of a privilege, toast and water has attractions which are incomprehensible to our maturer age. And Anne thoroughly appreciated toast-and-water, and showed it.

"You're drinking it all," remonstrated the invalid.

Anne shook her half-buried head. But when she put down the jug with a long breath, the remainder was so inappreciable that Henry's face fell.

"I think this is a stupid game," he said

sulkily. "I shan't play any more. *You* haven't got a cold, and it was you who gave me mine. What am I to do now, if my cough comes on?"

"There are the oranges," suggested Anne, consolingly. But the game seemed to have lost its interest for her too. She began to wander about the room in quest of more amusement for Henry and herself. But the room was exquisitely tidy with its Sunday tidiness, a Noah's ark, for the benefit of the twins, being the only hint of entertainment; and Anne never cared for Noah's ark, it did not leave enough to her imagination. She pulled all the animals out upon the floor, with a running commentary on their appearance the reverse of complimentary to the artist. Suddenly, as she was ranging the patriarch and his stolid family in a row before her, her evil genius inspired her with another bright idea.

"Oh, Henry, I have thought of a beautiful game now; it is quite a Sunday one, too."

"Play it by yourself, then," growled Henry, glancing malevolently at the jug, now lying suggestively on its side. "I don't want to play with silly little girls."

"Well, you needn't do anything. Just let me put that shawl over the pillows for a throne, and you can make yourself as comfortable as you like, and needn't move at all. Now, you are King Nebuchadnezzar. Sit still; only, when you begin to get very angry, you know, you must make yourself look different. Do you think you can? You don't often look different; that day you thought old Mr. Dobbins' big dog was coming after us you did, though," she added reflectively. "Somehow I don't think that would be exactly the right sort of face for Nebuchadnezzar either; but if you can't manage anything else, that will do. Now then, I am a big crowd. Here I come, dragging them along."

"What are you going to do?" asked Henry, with sudden anxiety.

" I'm going to play at the three men in the furnace. Look, there they are, just right; three of them, in their coats and in their hats, you know. There's a lovely fire, and as soon as I have brought them before you, I'm going to make it up. Seven times bigger it has to be; how big should you think that was? Half way up the chimney?"

" Indeed and indeed, Anne, you mustn't touch the fire. I mayn't go beyond the hearth-rug myself."

"I don't want you to. Of course the king wouldn't make up a fire for himself, not if he was ever so angry. I dare say he wouldn't know how, and it would be vulgar, wouldn't it? My mamma always says it is vulgar even to go into the kitchen, and it must be worse to do that."

"Anne, you must not play with the fire."

"It's not your fire, and I'm not your little girl."

"If you go any nearer to it I shall call for Mary Ann."

"You know she is out."

"There she is coming in!" exclaimed Henry in a tone of triumph, unwise, and premature. Indeed, at that moment the yard door was heard to open and a click of pattens came across the flags.

"She shan't come in here, then, if you scream the house down!" cried Anne, every instinct roused to revolt. And before Henry could stop her, or even guess her intention, she had sprung to the door, and, with some difficulty, turned the seldom-used key in the lock. She drew it out, flourished it once above her head, then, as he made a dart at it, dropped it deliberately inside her frock.

For one moment Henry glared at her in speechless indignation.

"Go on, do!" he exclaimed then. "Burn the house down if you like; only don't ask me to put it out. I won't be answerable for any single thing that happens any more."

He flung himself down on the sofa, turned his face to the wall, opened the *Youth's Magazine* with the air of a self-acquitted victim to human depravity, and —kept the tail of his eye fixed on Anne's proceedings with an expression betokening at least as much interest as disapproval. This is a humiliating confession for Henry's admirers; but after all, he was but human, and a human boy; he could not be altogether insensible to the charms of a good flare-up. Since there was no help for it, and he had protested, might he not indulge at least in a little curiosity?

Anne had set to work in a manner at once so business-like and so artistic as to suggest considerable acquaintance with the ways of fires. The coal-scuttle had unfortunately been left in the room, and the paper shavings from the Noah's ark assisted her unhallowed designs. In a very few minutes a good flare up had been indeed attained; long, aspiring, leaping yellow flame-monsters were rushing up the chimney with a sufficiently blood-curdling roar. Henry had turned round. Where now was the disapproval as compared with the genuine interest that shone in his once so languid eye? Alas! where? Dusty, coal-begrimed, crimson, the executioner stepped back, and surveyed her preparations with pardonable pride; too much excited even to notice the transformation in Henry, she pounced upon her stoically smiling victims.

"Ah-h!" she cried, "I'll teach you! Come on, now; see how you like this!"

The reality of the business now again flashed upon Henry.

"But Anne, you mustn't put in the Noah's ark men; they'll be burned."

"Of course they won't be burned!" retorted Anne, with exactly how much good faith let those who can remember an imaginative childhood say. "They are the three men in the furnace. You are a very wicked boy not to believe the Bible."

"But this isn't real," remonstrated Henry, fairly taken aback by this view of the question.

"You're a silly!" said Anne, and proceeded to the sacrifice.

Now, whether the weight of the victims disturbed the equilibrium of the fire, or whether a sudden draught from Anne's movements did the mischief, at that moment a large piece of paper was caught by the current and disappeared in a blaze of glory up the chimney. Half a minute, a minute, then a sudden, louder, and more ominous roar from above, a cloud of smoke, and a smothering smell of falling soot.

"Henry," said Anne very softly.

"Well?"

"Has this chimney been swept lately?"

The church-goers were nearly at their own gate, on the way home. The drizzling mist of the early afternoon had turned at last into a definite though quiet rain, and the family umbrella was in demand.

Now the family umbrella was an institution which did not admit of an extended view.

"How the blacks are flying!" said Mrs. Stephens, "and what a smell of soot. There must be a chimney on fire somewhere."

Captain Paton looked up from under his own umbrella to reconnoitre. Then he said, "Dear me!" Before Mrs. Stephens could ask the meaning of an ejaculation which was fairly equivalent to "good gracious," taking the tone into consideration, the piercing screams of Mary Ann rent the air, and Mary Ann in person had flung herself into Captain Paton's arms, gurgling hysterically—

"Oh, ma'am; oh, sir; the house is all ablaze from top to bottom, and the young lady and the young gentleman are being burned to death alive inside, this very blessed minute as ever is!"

CHAPTER IV.

THE WIDE, WIDE WORLD.

ALL the excitement was over; the quiet of the evening in both houses was as undisturbed as on any other Sunday. Hester was sleeping quietly beside Anne; only Anne herself lay hopelessly awake, despairing, miserable, smothering sobs in the bed clothes. The profound darkness which generally had no terrors for her, was full of awe that night; she thought it was her own iniquities that peopled it with indefinite horrors. In those days, still, children were practically supposed to be as innocent of nerves as an ascidian, and neither Anne herself, nor any one else, suspected that the events of the afternoon had given her a pretty severe shock. Yet she had been really frightened at the result of her realistic stage-management, more particularly in the moments that elapsed between the discovery that the door which had been difficult to lock was impossible to open, and the arrival of the rescue party.

The anger and reproaches which naturally followed an explanation were almost welcome at first, by comparison; but at last she began to feel worried, then despairing, then reckless, and conducted herself accordingly. Finally, she had been dismissed with a threat of punishment hanging over her head, more terrible than any present infliction. " I shall consider what must be done," Captain Paton had said, in a tone that lent impressiveness to the words. If the child could have known that the remark pointed to nothing worse than school, she might have been saved a good deal of imaginative suffering at the time, and much that happened in long after years might never have come to pass at all. The idea of being sent to school would have had no terrors for her; she was a sociable child who did not know what shyness meant, and though she might have rebelled against the sentence as a disgrace, when presented to her in the light of a penalty, she would have secretly looked forward to it as promising a certain amount of excitement. But, though this was indeed the whole meaning of Captain Paton's words, she did not know it; for though her parents had often discussed the matter before, with a sincere desire to do their best by their uncongenial child,

Anne had no idea that such a plan had ever occurred to any one.

There is always a certain terror in mere vagueness to the mind of an imaginative child; to this was added the torments of a child's conscience—pangs not to be measured by the mere discomfort attending the well-regulated remonstrances of the conscience of later life. What would happen to-morrow? it must be nearly to-morrow now. (It was about half-past nine.) And not only to-morrow, but the day after, and the day after that again? Could she ever get out of disgrace again? If it was not one thing it was another; there was no end to it. Why had not they let her go? Uncle Will would have been glad to have her. Oh, for somebody who would not be shocked at her; for a life in which Anne might be always Nancy, with all the privileges of lawlessness which she somehow associated with that name. How long the night was; should she ever go to sleep again? How dark! the darkness seemed to have swallowed her. And how quiet! Surely Hester must be more fast asleep than usual; not a movement, not a sound. She had gone to sleep with tears on her cheeks, poor Hester! partly for Anne's troubles, partly because Anne would not kiss good-night. She had spoken sharply, and pretended to be asleep when Hester called. That was long ago —hours and hours it must have been—and since then there had been this dreadful silence. Once, when she had quarrelled with Hester, she had been made to learn a poem about two little sisters who quarrelled, and before they made it up one died. Suppose—— A horrible dread took possession of her. She could not bring herself to call lest she should get no answer; her sobs stopped from mere excess of fear; she held her breath in an agony unspeakable that she might catch the sound of Hester's breathing, and the singing in her ears prevented her hearing it. Then, just as it was getting beyond endurance, there was a little sigh, a little stir; Hester moved slightly in her sleep. Anne cowered down again in a perfect ecstacy of relief. In the almost collapse that followed on that strain, sleep, despaired of, came, and when she next opened her eyes, lo! it was the grey dawn of to-morrow.

The question of what was to happen was not to be solved at once; only Anne found she was to be kept prisoner in a room apart, a room from which no friendly ivy offered the means of escape. She saw no Hester, neither did father nor mother disturb her solitude. Poor Mrs. Paton, indeed, was in bed with a nervous headache, due both to the fright of the preceding afternoon, and to a motherly heartbreak over the approaching separation from her ne'er-do-weel. For Captain Paton, for his part, had started already for Richmond, there to make arrangements for bestowing Anne in a seminary for young ladies, kept by a friend of the family. He was not really in such a desperate hurry to get rid of his daughter, but he had recollected that it was now close upon half-term, and the consideration appealed at once to his sense of order and to his instincts of economy.

The early morning hours passed on; from penitence Anne passed to anger, from anger to a wild defiance. She kicked and rattled at the door of her prison, but no one came, and the silent unemployed hours passed on till noon. Then the door was unlocked, and a maid brought in her dinner. Anne had no right from theory or prescription to expect anything more festive than bread and water, and she was a little surprised to see a repast in providing which her tastes might almost seem to have been particularly consulted. Indeed, so they had been; with that sentence of separation hanging over them, her mother, not without a pang of conscience, but gathering courage from the absence of her husband, had worked her poor throbbing brain to an unusual extent to order that dinner for the poor little prodigal, who was to be sent into the cold world to learn repentance. But Anne, little accustomed to such attentions, never suspected this.

"Mistress says that as soon as you've finished your dinner you are to take half an hour's walk in the garden, Miss Anne.

You are to walk up and down the middle path of the kitchen garden, so as cook can see you from the window all the time."

As Anne's heart secretly leaped within her at the news, of course she replied: " I shan't."

"Oh, fie, Miss Anne! aren't you ashamed to be such a naughty child again?"

Anne vouchsafed no answer, and the maid retired. When she came back with Anne's outdoor garments Hester crept in behind her, silent as a shadow. Poor Hester! she had caught rumours of the destiny which awaited Anne, rumours which had never reached the culprit herself, and her pretty eyes were swollen and red with crying.

" Oh, Anne! dear, dear Anne, it will be too dreadful; how will you bear it? I have been crying about it all the morning, dear. I suppose it can't be cruel of papa, because it is wicked to be cruel, and papa is good; but I don't know how he can bear to do this!"

"To do what?" was the question of Anne's mind. But pride and dread both kept her silent; she turned a little pale and her heart beat quicker, but no words passed her lips.

"Ah, Miss Anne, you see one can do a thing once too often. My! but this is bad," echoed Betsy, no less enigmatical and more ominous. "Well, I'm thinking you had better take your walk now, while you can get one."

A warder encouraging a criminal to his latest breakfast could scarcely have spoken in a different tone. What Anne suspected from it, would be hard to say. But somehow the very excellence of her dinner suddenly acquired something ominous; there was the queerest jumble in her mind of fattening up for ogres and yet of a solemn farewell to all dinners for an indefinite period. Neither sister nor maid guessed the extent to which she had been frightened. But when she passed quietly out into the garden she might have been a little Quaker ghost, in her grey frock, and the old black cape and bonnet, the last relics of mourning for old Mr. Paton, so sober was her demeanour, so pale the angel face just lighted up by those stray gold locks under her bonnet. But in her heart was the resolution at once of a great rebellion and of a great despair. Down the middle walk she went, and up again, the very picture of demureness. In vain did whole families of snails spread their attractions in her path; she ignored those illegal friends with the cool oblivion of a Henry the Fifth. Cook sat darning at the kitchen window; when Anne reached the medlar tree, half way down, where a few more or less damaged fruits lay in the soft mud, she looked up prepared for remonstrance. It was unneeded; Anne passed on with the air of one whom the vanities of life can no longer even tempt. Two more turns up and down; under this unwonted propriety her heart was beating more and more wildly. Would cook never move? Yes, at last; thinking vigilance wasted on Anne in her present mood, the watcher rolled up the stockings, took up her workbasket and disappeared. That was Anne's moment. With the agility of a monkey she scaled the back wall of the garden by means of the climbing fruit trees, descended by the ivy on the other side, and stood in the back lane unobserved and free.

It was but for a moment she stood, then she flew noiselessly down the road. There was no one in the lane, she fled on unseen, devoid of any plan of action, only knowing that she was going to Uncle Will. There were fields the other side of the road ; she got over the first stile and ran just inside the hedge so long as her breath held out. By degrees she began to slacken her pace. The rain had passed over; St. Luke's summer had come with a misty brightness ; the shadows of the fading elm trees in the hedgerow seemed to lie asleep across the damp fading grass. It was not proper country, yet it was not town. It was a patient attempt at the pastoral under severe discouragement, but Anne had always held it to be country.

The largeness of the world had never so impressed itself upon her before. She moved along in a kind of dance—some sort of dancing movement was always more natural to her than walking; but for fear of detection she would have sung.

The colour had come back to her cheek; in utter luxury of recklessness she snatched off her bonnet, and danced on, swinging it in her hand. The first breath of freedom had swept away all the terror and despair, there remained only the first tumultuous joys of successful revolt. She seemed at once to be friends with the whole world, of kin to nature. The sparrows in the hedge nodded to her with a kind of free and easy freemasonry, the very rustling of dried leaf and twig, the faint whisper of the breeze, had secrets for her, none the less thrilling because she never exactly discovered what they were. Surely the tramp, like the poet, is born, not made. What vagabond instinct, derived from what far-off ancestors—ancestors whose claim to the veneration of their posterity did not at all lie in their respectability—was stirring in their unconscious descendant then? But when the first ecstacies were over, Anne began to reflect that if Uncle Will was to be reached, and with him perpetual liberty, she must be practical. She calculated that some time would elapse before she would be missed, but before then she must be beyond reach of tracking or pursuit. How this was to be accomplished she had very little idea. Perhaps she meant to lie hidden in some pathless jungle of blackberry bushes while the cry and trampling of the chase swept unsuspecting past her hiding-place. But fortune or fate had better precautions in store for her.

The fields ended at last in three cross-roads, and at the cross-roads there stood an inn, quite a pseudo-country inn, like all the rest. Here was the first danger from human beings which had yet come in Anne's way. She crouched down behind the hedge to reconnoitre. Voices came through the open door, but no one was to be seen. At the door stood a horse and a covered cart; the horse, fastened by the bridle to a hook in the wall, had been left unwatched—the owner was probably refreshing within. Spite of the very original spelling, Anne made out that the cart was the property of William Higgins, carrier. Between what places he carried she neither knew nor cared; for her all roads led to liberty; the horse's head being turned away from Clapham, it sufficed her. Quivering with excitement, she rose from her concealment, stood a moment irresolute, then, darting across the road, scrambled into the cart, and in an instant was hidden among the packages and boxes at the back.

Light though she was, her sudden entrance had disturbed the horse a little;

it moved uneasily, trampled, and pulled upon the bridle, the clumsy wheels creaking as the cart shook. The movement seemed to rouse William Higgins to a sense of business, for shortly afterwards he came out and resumed his seat. Anne, in her dark corner, held her breath in a momentary agony of suspense, but he did not even look round as he hoisted himself to his place.

They were off. Not rapidly, indeed, but off they were, and as the slow steady jog carried her further and further out into the unknown, Anne began to breathe more freely. It is true she was not comfortable physically. Several hanks of yarn were tickling her face; the sharp corner of a box of groceries dug into her shoulder at every rougher jolt. The space into which she had crept was only about half large enough for her, so that even her supple young limbs got stiff and cramped at last. Yet she did not mind. She did not dare to make any considerable change in her position for fear of noise, but she moved her head cautiously, so as to get a back view of the driver between the boxes. She hoped to be able to guess whether he was a kind man, likely to be forgiving, perhaps even helpful in the event of discovery. But though there was a vague suggestion of vegetative content about that back view, she did not get much satisfaction from it, on the whole.

She could not at all tell in what direction, or through what country, they were going. At long intervals she heard the heavy trot of a horse, or the rumble or rattle of wheels, but that was all. Now and then the bough of a tree stretching across the road came into sight; such glimpses had all the excitement of incidents. Once, after some two hours' journey, they drew up. Anne was seized with a panic, thinking it might mean a search among the packages; but it proved to be only a toll-bar, and in a few moments they were jogging on as before. On and on, till at last, from the monotony of enforced silence and immobility, she fell asleep, restlessly at first, and rousing with uncomfortable starts, but at last, in spite of cramp and discomfort, she slept as soundly as ever she had done in her little bed at home.

Some two hours later, again, a sudden paroxysm of jolting woke her with a start from a troubled dream. She had a nightmare of big rocks just tumbling on her head, and, even as she woke, the dream was fulfilled. With an irrepressible scream —and she could scream—Anne disappeared beneath a hamper of good things destined for Master James Goodchild at Dr. Twiggs' academy, Guildford. Betrayal was bad, but not so bad as annihilation, and her first shriek of instinct was followed by a series of muffled cries for assistance. But assistance did not come, though the cart had stopped; for, at the sound of the first cry, William Higgins, answering it with a yell of terror, had fled for dear life towards the nearest cottage, carrying an urgent appeal for help and a blood-curdling narrative. Therefore it came to pass that Anne, having with some difficulty extricated herself, climbed out as unseen as she had climbed in. By the time the carrier returned with a couple of sturdy labourers armed with pitchforks and other defences against the supernatural, the little grey ghost was already some distance away.

They emptied the whole cart, ransacked every corner, and examined all boxes and hampers that admitted of examination, but of course they found nothing. Then one of the men reminded the other that it was close here that the pedlar's body had been found four years previously. The other man, though admitting that the pedlar walked, inclined to hold him guiltless of this particular disturbance, as, though he had often been seen, he had never been heard. His own opinion was that it had been a warning. With some folks it was knockings; with others, music; with others, again, screechings, like this here. And such was a very sure kind. Dogs was sure, and death-ticks was sure. But *they* might be heard by anybody, so to say, and mean somebody else all the time. These sorts *always* was for the party as heard them; well, for him, or some of his nearest folk. To the tune of these cheering remarks the cart was reloaded, and the carrier proceeded on his darkening way, a wiser but a sadder man.

But Anne, too, was feeling the first horrors of eeriness creeping over her with the creeping shadows. The catastrophe had taken place at the foot of a small hill covered with a young plantation of spruce firs. Into this she had crept through a gap in the hedge, and there she had the resolution to wait till the cart went on again. But the duskiness, peopled as it seemed with ghostly stems, appalled her. It was barely six o'clock, but the sun had lately set, and that makes night to a child. Moreover, it had gone down in clouds; no after-glow brightened the sky and prolonged the day. A chill air stole insidiously through her inappropriate clothing. Anne began to shiver with cold, and fear made her yet chiller. She hurried on nervously and painfully to escape from the uncanny wood, where goblin legs stretched out suddenly to trip her up, and goblin arms made snatches at her as she passed.

Out of the wood she did get at last. But even then she felt little inclination to whistle, if whistling implies cheerfulness, for she did not feel cheerful at all. Standing, as she did, at the very top of a hill, she could see the wide, wide world before her, and she felt unutterably unprotected and forlorn. By daylight it was as fair a view as need be wished, with its varied woods and pastures, and far blue stretches of undulating land, the most homelike of farm houses peeping out here and there among the trees. But now it was the dreariest period of dusk. The fields stretched out before her grey and colourless, the woods looked only dreary forests, while the ruddy glow from cottage hearths, which is conventionally supposed to cheer the wanderer at this hour, was conspicuous by its absence. So she stood desolate on the hill top, shivering in the falling dew, face to face for the first time in her life with the question of supper and bed, and finding no answer in either case. The fields certainly promised least of all in that direction, so she climbed the first gate that offered and found herself in the high road again. She walked on, but how differently! Worn out, heart and body, she sat down at last upon a mile-stone, and watered the dust of the world's highway with her tears.

"So! softly, softly! what's the matter with the old girl?"

The post-chaise had come close up to her before she perceived it; the horse shying violently at the mysterious figure on the mile-stone was the first thing to startle her, and she screamed out. The driver sprang down to quiet the horse, while his companion looked through the deepening twilight for the cause of the disturbance.

"Well, what was it? The pedlar's spirit, or a spirituous pedlar? Why, it's a little girl!" He too jumped out with a sort of good-natured curiosity. "Crying too! Beauty and innocence in tears; the orphan and the post-chaise.

> "'What are you doing, child, I said,
> By night along these lonesome ways?'"

"Oh, please," sobbed Anne, "I wasn't doing any harm. I'm Anne Paton, and they didn't want me at home, because I'm such a naughty girl, so I'm going to Uncle Will, and please is this the road to Brighton, and where is Uncle Will?"

The young man gave a long whistle, between amusement and dismay.

"Paton did you say? And you are going to your uncle? You poor little beggar!" He stood staring at her in much perplexity till the driver called out that they would be late, and the horse was getting cold. "What am I to do? I can't leave her here all night, and I have no means of sending her back. It will be out of the frying-pan into the fire to take you on, Miss Anne; still, scramble up there, so; I'll see you safe into Uncle Will's hands. George will see that you come to no great harm, I suppose, and the dowager will mother you to the best of her ability, and if that doesn't happen to be much, George will show her. She is a docile pupil, is the dowager; but forgetful, strangely forgetful."

"Do you know my cousin George?" asked Anne, languidly curious, but too sleepy, hungry, yet relieved, to feel much surprise.

"I have known him since I was about

as tall as that whip, and he was a fractious baby, or a very little old man, I scarcely know which; a parchment coloured creature, all wrinkles and scarlet hair. We hated each other in those days, and we each had some right on our side. He was my rival, you see; till he came I had been leading juvenile, as it were, but he quite cut me out. And I don't think he can have loved me. At that period the height of my ambition was to be a clown, and whenever I had a chance I used to get him to rehearse with."

"I don't understand about that," said Anne with a sigh. Such a new and wonderful world seemed opening out to her. "Are you a relation?" she asked, with a sudden hope.

"Oh, no! I am only Charles, his friend."

"I wish you had been. I like you, Mr. Charles."

"Thank you. In the interests of truth, I should perhaps mention that Charles is not my name, it is only my title."

"What is your name?"

"My name is Horatio Valentine."

"How lovely! I didn't know there were such beautiful names anywhere in the world."

"I'm glad you like it; it would scarcely have been my own choice, but my dear mother's acquaintance with Shakespeare was slightly superficial. She thought the names sounded well together; alas! she forgot what a fall was there from Valentine, to Timbs."

"Well, I think Paton *is* prettier than that. But Mr. Hor——"

"Pardon the interruption, but I would really rather be Mr. Charles."

"Very well," said Anne, but regretfully. "I hate my own name, at least I used to.

You called me Miss Anne, just now, and I rather liked that; I don't know why, for it is just what nurse says twenty times a day. But that was not so bad as 'dear Anne.' That is what Henry Stephens calls me."

"Happy Henry," murmured Mr. Charles —for practice sake.

"Do you think so? I think he is miserable. If you only knew how stupid he is, and how he likes best to be stupid. Why, he wouldn't see the least fun in all this. I think he is the most miserable boy, and I am the happiest little girl. Oh, I am glad I came. What delightful things have happened already! I have had a ride in a cart, and another ride in a chaise, and met you, and not had to come in to tea, and been up hours after dark. And perhaps if they haven't room for me at Uncle Will's, I may have to sleep on two chairs, or even on the table! I think it has been the very nicest day of my whole life."

She ended with a little sigh of supreme content, and lay still for a while. Presently she asked sleepily—

"Is it far still to Brighton?"

"Well, rather. What made you think of going to Brighton?"

"Uncle Will said he was going there. Oh!" in sudden terror, "aren't you taking me to him? Isn't my Uncle Will the same as yours, after all?"

"Oh, yes; there's no mistake. It is true the company is going to Brighton, eventually, but at present it is no nearer that than Guildford. I should have been with it, but I had to wait in London a day or two on business of my dad's. He's the manager. I assure you it is all right. Alas! you doubt me still?"

"No, I don't doubt you, Mr. Charles."

She felt for his hand with her little cold one. Then she nestled down into his unaccustomed arms as happily as if he had been Uncle Will himself, and fell asleep. Fortunately, Mr. Timbs was a versatile genius. He resigned himself with a good grace to his new rôle, and bore the constraint of motionlessness with creditable patience for the rest of the drive.

CHAPTER V.

COUSIN AND AUNT.

THE coffee-room of the Stag Inn, at Guildford, was quite full that night. The company that filled it was tolerably miscellaneous looking; but they all seemed thoroughly to understand how to make themselves comfortable according to their own ideas. The attitudes even of the ladies, of whom there were two or three, were, as a rule, more distinguished for ease than elegance. One end of the table was covered with the remains of a nondescript sort of meal; there was a round of cold boiled beef, cheese, pickles, and gooseberry jam, while a teapot and cups mingled with pewter mugs and tumblers, suggestive of stronger beverages, of which, indeed, the fragrance still lingered lovingly about the room. This was in course of being superseded by the pungent odour of tobacco smoke, but nobody seemed to object to either.

Though comfortable, the society did not seem to be particularly amused, and there was a movement of satisfaction such as suggests the lower depths of dulness, when wheels were heard clattering over the stones of the court-yard below. A large, florid man, who had been studying the county paper threw it down with an air of some relief.

"That's Horry, at last," he announced; and a general brisking up replied to his words. "Well, my boy," as his son entered elaborately; then, "What on earth have you got in those rugs?"

Horatio smiled mysteriously; then he

sat calmly down before the fire holding his burden still covered up. Anne, in fact, was still sleeping, too thoroughly exhausted to be easily awakened.

"Ladies and gentlemen," he said, "it would gratify me to allay your curiosity. But the claims of friendship are paramount, and there may be reasons why—ahem! I say, George, shall I tell them?"

"What are you talking about?" A tall lad rose from a seat in a far off corner where he had been studying a small book by the light of a solitary candle. He replaced the book in his pocket as he came forward.

"What was that? Slowbore on book-keeping, or Diddler on stocks? And then to think of what I have here! Could I have believed it one short hour ago? Oh! George, as a true friend and mentor, I must tell you you are beginning much too early."

"These remarks strike one as singularly destitute of point, even for you."

"Ah! the point, that is here," said Charles, his friend, bestowing a cautious pat on his bundle. "All the way from Clapham for the sake of your *beaux yeux*; and but for me—it—might never have reached you at all. And this is friendship, this is gratitude!"

George Paton turned on his heel with an impatient gesture of contempt.

"Never mind the Don, Charles; if he doesn't think it advisable to be interested we are."

"On his head then be the responsibility of the revelation," said Horatio solemnly. "Unveil my sleeping beauty! So. By Jove you *are!*"

He had not seen his charge before so as to distinguish her, and her beauty fairly took him by surprise. Her bonnet had fallen off, the loveliest flush was on her cheeks, and as they crowded round to look at her, her eyes opened, deepened with sleep, widened with perplexity.

"Where am I? Hester, oh, Hester!" she exclaimed, and then memory came back to her. She knew now where she was, but too bewildered yet to speak she sat on Mr. Timbs' knee, staring in silence at the group around her.

"Who is she?" "Where did you find her?" "George, you lucky young rascal, I congratulate you." "What eyes!" "There's a turn of the head for an exit!" "Oh, you little darling dear! I must kiss her, Mr. Timbs, I must indeed."

This from a gushing young lady who had taken the *ingénues* for a number of years, which only the spiteful cared to compute. Suiting the action to the word she pushed through the group, and kneel-by Horatio's side flung her arms round the darling dear, and was about to honour her with a rapturous salute. The sequel was rapid. Anne, scared, worn out, stared out of countenance, saluted Miss Clarke with a vigorous box on the ear, and amidst a roar of delight hid her head on her protector's breast in a storm of sobs.

"You said you would take me to Uncle Will! Where is Uncle Will? I won't be kissed by a lot of horrid old women. I thought you were nice! Oh! why did I ever come? Papa, papa, take me back, and I'll never be naughty again."

Mr. Timbs' expressive countenance betrayed a certain amount of discomposure; before he could quite recover his presence of mind George came striding up.

"Who is this child?" he said sharply.

Horatio meekly explained.

"You idiot! what made you bring her here?"

"So young and yet so hard! I knew the bonds of friendship sat lightly on your soul, but I thought you might still be sensible to the claims of kindred. I supposed you would see to her, of course."

"I?"

"Well," said the other, his usually fine temper giving way a little, "you or your governor."

George deigned no reply in words, nor were words necessary. He turned abruptly to the child, who was still crying quietly, though interest and curiosity were fast drying her tears, and took her in his arms.

"Come, Anne," he said, "you are overtired. Come with me, and my mother shall give you some tea and find you a bed."

"Ay! marry, that *shall* she indeed!"

cried out his irrepressible friend. Perhaps it was something of a Parthian shot, for George bit his lip as he heard it; but he took no further notice and departed, with Anne's head resting confidingly upon his shoulder.

The others were left to chaff Anne's unlucky knight to their heart's content.

"Poor Charles! I always feared you would catch a Tartar."

"Oh! Charles, I thought you were nice!"

"Are you going to break her in yourself? There will probably be various breakages in your own person before you have finished, but don't despair. Faint heart—you know!"

"Rubbish!" exclaimed the persecuted champion, "she'll go back to-morrow. I say, what a lovely little termagant it is!"

"Don't think of it, my dear fellow; be

sure the Don has made the running already."

"Yes, the sudden revelation of your charms, it must have startled her. That was it, my poor Mokanna!"

This last from his father; and the rest, who might not perhaps have ventured it on their own account before their manager, roared appreciation. Certainly, if masculine beauty is, in truth, a factor of any great importance in the eyes of ladies, other than those of the heroines of novels and their biographers, Horatio would all his life stand a poor chance beside his friend. He was hideous, with the grotesque hideousness of a gurgoyle. Lean, lantern-jawed, and ill-complexioned, he had no graces of form to atone for deficiencies in feature, for he was stooping, overgrown and shambling, looking as though his limbs had come together by accident, and had never got accustomed to one another yet. Spite of all which he was, and always would be, ten times more popular with man, woman, and child than was George Paton, who looked as if he might have walked out of a canvas of Giorgione, and was merely masquerading in nineteenth century clothes, yet rather to their glorification than to his detriment.

As he stood for a moment at the door of his mother's room, Anne contemplated him in the dim lamp-light with a certain amount of awe. For the first time in her life she saw an imposing face and figure. She had seen many that tried to be so, but it had been half an imposition, half a failure; here she found it, not sought after but inevitable—here in this boy, too precocious by far, his elders said, for already only on the borders of seventeen he had something of the dignity of manhood, and no one could deny it. Her red-haired cousin! The little parchment coloured old man! The complexion was pale, indeed, but ivory would have been a fitter comparison; the red hair had deepened into chestnut, too pronounced to be commonplace. Neither curly nor wavy, there was a sort of severity about its straightness which set off better than wave or curl, the severe beauty of form for which his head was remarkable. Perhaps at this period of his life severity was the most noticeable feature of his whole bearing and expression.

George's rap was repeated with some impatience, superadded to its peremptoriness, and this time a voice which seemed to belong to someone in a chronic state of unreadiness, entreated for one moment. The request was granted with the most literal exactitude, for the next moment George did open the door.

Anne was aware of a sort of ponderous flutter, a little moan of "Oh, George," and saw a stout and comely woman, with rumpled hair of a brighter shade than her son's, rise from her seat on the edge of a rumpled bed, and make a frantic clutch at the unloosed fastenings of a rumpled dressing-gown. The next moment she was snatched from his arms and folded to the ample bosom of Aunt Theresa, nor did she resent this embrace. George gave briefly the introduction which had not been asked for, but which was acknowledged by a yet more vigorous squeeze, and then Mrs. William Paton sat down with her on the bed again, and Anne had leisure to look about her.

The bed-room was in a state of the most glorious untidiness; indeed the untidiness attained to such colossal and unique proportions, that it almost seemed a work of genius. No ordinary mind could have evolved such a mess out of such limited materials. Every available article was not only in the wrong place, but in the most wrong place that could possibly be. A hair-brush was fraternizing with a tea-cup in the easy-chair; a bonnet was the most conspicuous article on the tea-tray which had been balanced across the water-jug; the grim solid-looking furniture seemed to have been suddenly arrested in the midst of a game of "general post." Even Anne, who professed to love disorder, felt more bewildered than delighted; George wrenched round one or two of the dissipated looking chairs into decorous angles with an exclamation of disgust.

"Well, George, I know it isn't quite tidy," said his mother apologetically; "but if you had given me a minute or two, I was just going to put it straight."

"I can do it," said George; then, with sudden recollection, "mother, this child is tired out and half starved; hadn't you better ring for some fresh tea and some bread-and-butter? Or, stay—nobody ever answers this bell, I will go and see about it myself. I dare say Anne would like to brush her hair and put herself tidy," he added.

His tone was fraught with awful meaning, but the implied rebuke was not aimed chiefly at his abashed cousin. She, for her part, felt small to a degree, but the chief culprit only smiled benevolently as she hugged her niece anew.

"We will both be fit to receive the Holy Father himself by the time you come back," she said cheerfully. "One moment, George; was your father in the coffee-room?"

"He has not been there all the evening."

"Well, then, my dear, I dare say you may find him somewhere about. Be sure you tell him about this sweet little visitor; say how Anne has come all this way to see her dear uncle; tell him he must be sure to come up at once or we shall be dreadfully angry."

The verbal message was supplemented by a whole torrent of winks, becks, and nods to which George answered with a concentrated frown.

"How could you let him go?" he burst out.

"I couldn't help it; really, George, you expect impossibilities. You know your poor father never could stand dulness, and this is the dullest town I ever was in. A man will amuse himself somehow, and there's many men I could name worse; I'm sure no one ever knew *him* spoil a part. And to-night—he can't have been gone very long, and a good chance of getting him away at once. You will, won't you, dear?"

"I shall do what I can for the best," said George, darting a look of warning towards Anne. But she had heeded little of the conversation. In no case could it have conveyed the slightest suspicion to her mind; but this, George, with his sadly precocious enlightenment on many subjects —enlightenment so precocious that he sometimes felt as though he must have been born knowing—would never have believed.

Left to themselves, the aunt and niece soon became the fastest friends. Mrs. William tidied up the room, Anne, and herself, in a fragmentary sort of way, giving a touch to each as the thought struck her. Could it have been but two nights ago that Anne had rebelled at putting back her chair against the wall after tea, and undergone all the tortures of a brisk toilet at the hands of her nurse? Aunt Theresa's soft lazy touches were as new as they were delicious.

For all George's presumable vigour, tea must have been a long time coming, for by the time it made its appearance, even this desultory tidying had effected something approaching to order. Mrs. William had squeezed herself with undisguised reluctance into a flowery gown, whose deficiencies were not glaringly apparent, and scrambled up her hair under an all-concealing cap. To do it elaborately indeed would have been no slight undertaking. It was many years since Theresa Paton had had any claims to be considered a young woman; but many young women might have envied her hair still. It was so much brighter than George's that it only just escaped being aggressively red, but the mass of it was marvellous. To her niece, of course, Aunt Theresa was an old lady, and her looks no more worthy of consideration than those of other old ladies. Yet she was a fine woman still; rather in the Rubens style now, but it was quite possible that she might once have been beautiful with a beauty rather splendid than refined.

Tea came at last, but George did not accompany it, rather to Anne's relief. The meal, without the restraint of his presence, seemed to her the most delicious she had ever tasted. Her spirits rose; she chattered and laughed. Mrs. Paton plied her with questions about home; she answered with indifference, not being troubled with home-sickness as yet. But she was astonished to find how much this quite unknown aunt knew about them, and said so at last.

"Why, my dear, Mr. Paton has always felt very kindly to your good papa, very; as for there ever having been any quarrel that is just talk. There never was anything of the sort between the families, never. Our ways of life are different, and that has kept us apart, that is all. As for your dear mamma, I was quite looking forward to seeing her myself the day your uncle called last week, but George thought it better not."

"Why didn't Cousin George want you to go?"

"Well, he was rather annoyed when he found how your uncle had made himself up. It was a pity he came to know of it; he never quite understands that sort of thing. We meant to keep it quiet, but I had forgotten to lock my door at the last —I quite thought I had done so—and just as he came in your uncle was jagging up his boots a bit with a table knife, and I was rolling up the bolster in a shawl (I was to have come with a baby tied on my back, my dear, like the women in pictures). And he got to the bottom of it all in a moment, he is so quick, and he seemed so put out about it that I gave it up."

"Were you disappointed?"

"My dear, I think I cried a bit when your uncle had gone. It would have been such fun, and I had taken such pains. You thought your uncle looked the part well, didn't you? but it was only half the show without me. However, it was not worth while making George unhappy about. He can't understand how these little jokes are all so much pleasantness between brothers and sisters. Bless me! such tricks as we all used to play off on one another when we were boys and girls together; if we could meet now I don't know that we are quite too sorry and sober for the old ways still. But I don't know where to lay hands on one of them —those that are left; we never were great folks for writing, any of us," she said cheerfully.

Anne's curiosity was greatly roused.

"Then if you had brothers and sisters you must have had a father and mother, because if you had all come *loose*, you see, how could you have known you belonged to one another?"

"What do you mean?"

"Why I mean if you had been just *made*, like—like the tadpoles," said Anne, selecting the being whose genesis was to her at once the subject of deepest interest and of darkest mystery. "I heard mamma say, 'nobody knew whether you ever had a father or mother.'"

"Oh!" said Jane Paton's sister-in-law

with unruffled temper; "but that was only a way of speaking. My mother was Irish, and we mostly favoured her, though I sometimes think George must have taken after my father. I scarcely remember him; he was an Italian, that's how I came to be called Theresa. I believe he had got into trouble in his own country, and could never go back. I often think, Nan," she added reflectively, "what would all poor foreigners do without England?" She evidently looked upon her unknown father as some one quite disconnected with herself, a poor and not too creditable exile whom her mother had generously taken in and done for by marrying him.

"Have I any other cousins except Cousin George?" asked Anne.

"No, my dear; you ought by rights to have had nine, eight more that is; but I never could make them do well."

"Oh! Aunt Theresa, how nice if they could have lived. Was George the eldest?"

"No; he came—let me see—yes it was sixth. There were the twins first. I'm not finding fault with the ways of Providence, but it did seem hard to have begun with twins. Nineteen years old I was, nineteen and a month, not a day more. Well! the saints know I did my best for you, my blessed jewels; but they died, of course. Beatrice pined from the first, and Benedict somehow tumbled off the sofa one day when I was getting up in a hurry, and it seemed to touch him in the head. He cried for about a week, night and day, and then he had fits, and so he died. We were at Norwich then, and they are buried there. It shows you what a wandering life I have had, my dear; those two are the only ones out of all the eight that are buried in the same place. One is at Durham, another at Exeter; my angel Mike—the last he was—is at Lynn. That's not so far from his brother and sister as some of them."

Anne listened intently, and child though she was almost wondered; there was such cheerful resignation, yet such indubitable affection, in the tone of these reminiscences. Time, indeed, had healed her wounds in one way; perhaps George had contributed unconsciously to heal them in another. For though she was not only content but proud to live under his adored despotism, yet she was in a way deposed from motherhood, so far as he was concerned. But the eight dead babies, to them she was a mother still; they clung about her for ever with phantom embraces which they would never grow too old to dispense with; she hushed their voiceless wailings, and they smiled on, through all her wildest aberrations of dress and manners. They never looked a reproach, though indeed their early deaths lay chiefly at her door, for she had been the best meaning and the most incompetent of mothers. One after another those infants had succumbed to sheer ill-treatment. Not vulgar brutality, such as brings certain abnormal monstrosities into a police-court. On them no touch save in the way of kindness had ever been laid. They were only starved spasmodically, from pure forgetfulness, and such lapses of memory were atoned for by a proportionate rush of plenty. Nevertheless they died—of late hours, of unsuitable food, of irregularities of every description —died as it were worn out by dissipation, at ages varying between six weeks and three months. It is probable that George owed his life less to the inherent vigour of his constitution than to the fact that circumstances had deprived him of his mother's baleful care till he had attained an age when the worst dangers of infancy were long past. In fact he was twelve years old before he ever made his parents' acquaintance. Mrs. William had just begun a history of the circumstances when the hero of the tale himself entered the room.

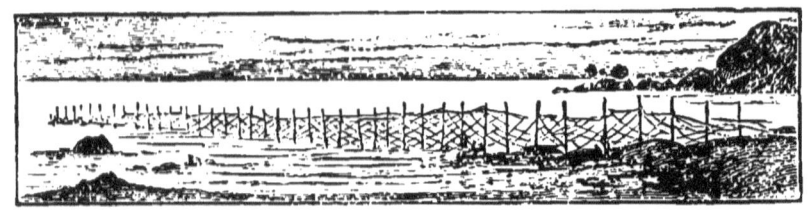

CHAPTER VI.

THE FAMILY SKELETON COMES OUT OF THE CUPBOARD.

GEORGE'S very look as he came in was enough to check at once his mother's flow of anecdote.

"Your father?" she said nervously.

George made a gesture of despair.

"What could you expect?" he asked almost fiercely. "There, don't cry," he went on more gently; "that's no use now. I blame myself most. And he is not at his worst, one may say that."

"Really not? You're not just saying so to comfort me?" she said, checking her tears as easily as she had produced them.

"What would be the use of doing that? No; he is quite quiet, if that is all, but—— Good Heavens! mother, isn't that child gone to bed?"

Mrs. Paton jumped up guiltily, more or less tumbling Anne out of her arms on to the floor, and the two stood staring, the one helplessly, the other gloomily, at the bewildered child, who stood uncomprehending before them.

"I didn't know where to put her," faltered her aunt. "I'm afraid I forgot all about it. Oh, George, what am I to do?"

"Put her—oh, put her anywhere; my room if there is nowhere else. I can sleep with Charles, or on the sofa in the coffee-room, or on the billiard-table, if that's all; what does it matter? Only pray take her away at once. Would you have the child see him?"

"Who am I not to see? Oh, Aunt Theresa, I came to see Uncle Will."

"Yes, dearie, and so you shall," said her distracted guardian; "to-morrow morning. But it is time now for all good little girls to be in bed. George, I don't like that plan; I know you won't really go to Charles, and——"

A step and a voice, at the far end of the passage.

"Too late!" he exclaimed. "Now manage it yourself. Oh, mother, mother!"

There was a sound of wringing of hands in his voice, but in this last emergency his mother recovered her presence of mind, and soared boldly on the wings of fiction.

"Nan, dear, I'm sorry to say your poor uncle is not at all well to-night; quite ill, isn't he, George?" she said, with vigorous suggestiveness. George bent his soul to sign the assent he would not speak. "You must be a good little girl, and not tease him to notice you, or—or—anything. Now mind!"

And, even as she spoke, George drew a deep breath and clenched his hands in impotent passion, for William Paton had come in.

Alas!

George had been right; he was far from being at his worst. He had, indeed, only reached the genial and sentimental stage, and was still just so much master of himself as to be hazily conscious of a need for exerting over his actions a power of control which was rapidly escaping him. He did not hazard himself far into the room, but stood by the door, smiling faintly in silence. His wife stood helpless; at heart she was a good deal relieved, for to her this did not seem much. George stood like an Indian at the stake, resolved only not to blench for the very worst that could befall. And from between the wife and son, on whom his vague benevolent glances beamed alternately, Anne ran towards him, innocent, pitying, sincere.

"Uncle Will!" she cried; "I am come to be your little Nan, after all. Oh! I forgot you were ill. Are you very bad? I won't tease you, I won't indeed; but just kiss me good-night, and say you are glad to see me after all!"

She held up her sweet face for his embrace, standing on tip-toe and holding by his arm. It was too much; George's stoicism broke down. He sprang forward with a smothered cry, and almost dashed the child back into the room. She stumbled and would have fallen, had not her aunt caught her. George did not even look to see what had become of her; at that moment he could almost have enacted

Virginius to save her from the profanation. Not that he cared for her; indeed he hated her then, as he had scarcely been stirred to hate before; hated her for being witness of a degradation which he felt as his own; yet more for her innocent unconsciousness of the shame which was burning into his very soul. Scarcely knowing what he did, he grasped his father's arm, so roughly that it was only not a blow, and seemed about to thrust him from the room.

"Oh, George, don't hurt him; remember he is your father," exclaimed Mrs. Paton. She was neither tearful nor hysterical, not excited in any way; the remark was merely an utterance of intercession. But George, colouring to the roots of his hair, loosed his passionate grasp and stepped back.

"I beg your pardon, father; I forgot myself," he said.

He spoke with deliberate clearness in a voice rather raised than subdued, and for the rest of the time he interfered neither by word nor act, but stood silent and motionless, not allowing himself to look away.

"Oh, my dear, I didn't mean that," said his mother, much more distressed at the atonement than at the crime, which, indeed, she had merely looked upon as a rather harsh exercise of legitimate authority.

But William Paton, suddenly roused to a bewildered sense of injury, tottered forward, and subsided into a chair and tears.

"Heaven help me! even my own children forsake me," he exclaimed, with more pathos than originality. "Never mind. Don't say anything. I deserve it. George, my boy, your poor old father won't trouble you long. I—shan't trouble any one long —not long—not—— "

" Hold your tongue, William, do," said his wife sharply. "Aren't you ashamed, before the child? Come along, Nan," she continued, suddenly remembering her explanation. "You see your poor dear uncle is too ill to talk to you to-night. You can't do him any good, dearie; there's only George and I understand his illnesses. Come along to bed, and to-morrow you shall see him quite a hearty, happy Uncle Will."

She was dragging the bewildered child from the room, but her fatally irrepressible husband broke out again.

"You too!" he exclaimed sepulchrally. "What! not a word? not a look? And is this the end?"

"No, no," cried Anne, breaking from her aunt's detaining hand. "Everyone else may leave you; other people"—with an indignant glance at George—"may be as horrid and unkind as they like; but I will always be your little Nancy! If you are naughty, you can put up with me; and I like naughty people best. Does your head ache too much to understand?" she said anxiously, a headache being her one idea of the ills that flesh is heir to.

"Bless you, my child, bless you," he wept. "The blessing of a weary pilgrim through this vale of tears, in which," he went on, irrelevantly but impressively, and quite oblivious of her existence, "the ways of Providence are no doubt mysterious, but they are good"—rapturously—"and to the humble believer who knows——"

An imploring glance from George sent Mrs. Paton out of the room with Anne before he had got further.

As awkward as it was ever in her easy-going nature to feel perhaps Theresa Paton felt then, as she hurried her niece along the passages to a rather dreary little inn bedroom, opposite George's, in a remote wing. Talking incessantly herself, to prevent the child talking, she scrambled her into bed as rapidly as she might, and went away with a sense of having escaped.

It was not she who came to the rescue an hour or two later when Anne woke, startled and screaming, to the moonlit awfulness of her first night of absolute solitude. She, by that time, was sleeping the sleep of the just, no anxiety as to her niece having so much as occurred to her. Yet Anne was not left unprotected. It was indeed rather a fresh horror than a comfort to her, at first, when the door opened, and a tall figure seemed to step in out of the darkness and come towards her. But it was only George. His consolations were not exactly sympathetic, but he was not harsh. He insisted on her defining what was the matter. She wanted Hester; she had dreamed she saw Hester somewhere in a lovely garden, and when she wanted to run and kiss her Hester had said, "Oh! Anne, you can't come." Then she woke up, and there was a horrid moon —Anne devoutly hated that admired luminary—and then she remembered that Aunt Theresa had never heard her say her prayers, and she was frightened.

George recognized the terrors of conscience, and with the readiness of one accustomed to every kind of emergency, he volunteered to help her remedy the omission, standing over her in the chill moonlight of the small hours, as she knelt up in bed and sobbed out after him some child prayer learned by him—but not from his mother—in his own infancy. If it was not exactly identical with her own form it satisfied her, and she ended quite consoled, and as a matter of course with a kiss which cost him more than anything else. Then, discovering her peculiar horror of moonlight, he darkened the window to the best of his power, and wrapping her in a shawl walked up and down with her, till, in ten minutes time, he could put her back, a dreamless bundle, among her pillows, and return to his self-imposed watch in his own room.

It cannot be said that any liking for Anne in particular, or even a fondness for children in general moved him in this matter. It was merely a sense of duty, to which a feeling of its being also a penance gave a certain not unpleasant zest. For he had been very much ashamed of his ebullition of temper towards his father, he always was very much ashamed but it had not cured him; and his mind was of the order that finds a genuine satisfaction in penance. He was particularly annoyed at having forgotten himself before Anne. No suspicion crossed his mind that she had not been scandalized at all; the fact was that, to her, he seemed rather older than his father and mother,—a being to whom authority had been committed by right divine. Had George known this, perhaps his conscience would have troubled him less, but neither did he suspect that Anne's disapproval was an extra stimulant to his penitence. At seventeen one is scarcely expected to know fully what a deal of human nature there is in mankind in general and in oneself in particular.

But the whole affair had certainly not tended to increase his love for his cousin, for whom, from the first, his sentiments had been rather the reverse of affectionate; and the reflection that her hours, as their guest, were numbered, came to him with a very healing and soothing power. He took early steps himself towards effecting this desired consummation, rightly judging that if the arrangements were left to his parents Anne's departure might be almost indefinitely postponed. He was prepared for objections and remonstrance, would admit of no difficulties, and was adamant to entreaties. His mother he overcame by a pathetic and highly imaginative description of the desolation in Anne's paternal halls; Anne herself he simply overawed, first from indignation to tears, and then from tears to quiescence. The whole business had been arranged irrevocably as fate, long before Mrs. Paton had contrived to get her niece and herself ready for the more or less perennial breakfast in the coffee-room, to which they straggled down somewhere about ten. The breakfast had a strong family resemblance to the supper of the night before, slightly re-arranged. Some of the company had breakfasted already, and the meal looked none the more inviting. It was a pouring day, moreover, so that those who had finished were hanging about the room, or strolled in and out, as fancy prompted; it was all really horribly uncomfortable, and calculated to cool the ardour of any merely romantic attachment to an ideal life of unconventional freedom. Mr. Timbs was talking politics, or rather submitting to be talked to by some low-spirited enthusiast; Horatio was superintending another youth, who was engaged in recording an uncomplimentary opinion of Guildford, in halting verse, on the window pane. Some of the ladies were frankly mending their husband's stockings, and these were the best off.

Under the circumstances, Anne naturally came in for a greater amount of attention all round than might otherwise have fallen to her share. In fact she was outrageously petted and flirted with, and it must be owned that, now that a night's rest had restored her spirits and temper, she rose to the occasion with an audacity and enjoyment which added greatly to the mirth of her audience. There was quite a rivalry for her favour, and she coquetted as though to the manner born. There was nothing particularly humorous or refined, perhaps, about the badinage on either side; the really remarkable thing about her was her readiness. Possibly, nay probably, education would polish her style; but there was a strong dash of populace in her organization, an hereditary taint which it would be difficult for any education entirely to get rid of. At bottom, in many ways, she was ingrainedly *peuple;* she had that vigour of emotional expression which laughs and cries, hugs, hits out, blesses, and vituperates, in the back regions of a fishing village or a seaport town.

George, looking on with as much disgusted disapprobation as though instead of nine she had been nineteen and his *fiancée*, merely added the joys of tormenting to the general amusement, seeing which he had the sense to withdraw, retreating in good order.

"There! Miss Anne, you have driven him away. Aren't you sorry now? Confess!"

"No," said Anne, with decisive frankness from her throne on the manager's knee; "I'm very glad. I don't like him. If it hadn't been for him I might have stayed here altogether."

"Going!" There was a chorus of regrets and protestations.

"*I* don't want to go; I don't know what they'll do to me when I get back," said Anne, with plaintive resignation. "But George wouldn't care—not if it was wild horses," she continued, with a vivid reproduction of the style of Mary Anne. "He said you had no place here for little girls; but I can do ever so many things— nice things, I mean, of your sort. I can whistle, and I can dance,—not a hornpipe, but I could learn anything; I like it. And I can sing."

"She can sing! Won't you give us a song?"

"Oh! yes; what shall I sing? There is, 'O, that will be joyful!' That's a nice tune, but I don't like it, because I always have to sing it with Henry Stephens when company comes. Bob—that's our boy, Mr. Graves' boy—taught me 'I loves a drop of good beer;' but Bob sings all queer, and I couldn't make it out very well. Then there's the Old Hundredth and 'Giles Scroggins' Ghost,' and 'Home Sweet Home' and 'Cruel Barbara Allen,' and—— Oh! I know plenty. Shall I sing you 'Barbara Allen'? I learned that from Emma; she was our nurse-maid before last. We're always changing our nurse-maids. That's because nurse is a treasure; I heard mamma say that was why, but I didn't understand. Shall I begin?"

They laughed, as they encouraged her with anticipatory applause; but after the first few notes they laughed no more, for, technically appreciative audience that they were, they felt themselves to be in the presence of genius. Yet she sang with a supreme unconsciousness of the effect she was producing, as indifferent to her theme as to her powers. Had the pathos, the manifold inflections, the intense dramatic suggestiveness of the performance been one shade less undeniably instinctive, it would have seemed purely mechanical, for she was as far from seeing any particular point or pathos in the song as ninety-nine children out of a hundred would be. The last note had scarcely died away when she burst out laughing.

"Isn't it funny?" she said cheerfully. "'Young man, I think you're dying!' I wonder if her mamma had never told her it was bad manners to make personal remarks? That's what they would tell me if I had said that to anybody."

It was a relief to the strange tension consequent on the performance, and every one laughed the louder for it. Then they made her sing again and again. In everything she sang there was the same instinctive dramatic power; it was even more striking than was the quality of her voice, which, of course, was merely that of a child, though it was exquisitely sweet, true, and fresh, and so flexible and sympathetic as to give promise of a remarkable future.

No wonder Mr. Timbs audibly ejaculated, "Opera!" He did not clasp her to his heart with tears in his eyes, as the discoverers of juvenile genius are generally represented as doing. He did not do this, because he was English, and because he was not troubled with enough genius himself to give him a fellow-feeling. But doubtless he groaned, in his managerial soul, at the perverse fate which had revealed such a treasure to him only to snatch it away.

As for Mrs. Paton, she sobbed or laughed as the sentiment required, and overwhelmed Anne with embraces. Horatio treated her to all the arts of fascination which singularly ugly men have so often notoriously possessed. Altogether, Anne was having a good time that morning—of a kind so utterly new to her, that it was little wonder that her excitable head was fairly turned.

It was turned, with the natural result. When, about noon, George came with wraps and provisions to carry her off, she flew into one of her fits of passion, clinging, sobbing, screaming, to the amusement of most people, the compassion of Aunt Theresa, and the intense disgust of George. For the first time he came across a creature on whom his arguments and commands made no impression at all; perhaps, in the sight of his discomfiture, some of the spectators tasted the sweetness of revenge. With Anne, anger, or strong emotion of any kind, was a sort of madness while it lasted; no one had any chance with her. So at last George was fain to carry her off bodily, kicking, struggling, protesting, and unvanquished.

The sight of the carriage effected more than all her cousin's exhortations. It seemed to sober her with a sort of shock; she grew quiet, and subsided into silent abysses of despair. She asked for no pity; she stood crushed and hopeless, submitting without a struggle to the half-scolding, half-sympathetic chamber-maid who was getting her ready for her journey, as she stood on the step of the side door of the inn. George stood silent also, recovering his own dignity and temper with an effort.

Just as she was ready, her escort, an ordinary, good-natured looking, commercial traveller, came out of the bar, followed by William Paton. No traces of indisposition were discoverable in Uncle Will. He might have had but dim recollections of his interview with his niece the night before, but the whole situation had since been carefully explained to him by his wife, so that he showed no surprise either at her appearance or her departure. Of course, this cost him no pang whatever; in fact, he had insisted, quite as strongly as George, on her immediate return. But Anne could not believe that his anguish at the separation was one whit less poignant than, for the moment, was her own.

"I couldn't help it, Uncle Will," she whispered, as he took her in his arms. "Oh! I would have stayed with you if I could."

She clung to him with a desperation that made her quiver. He was really more amused than touched, but was too good-natured to let her think so.

"Never mind, Nancy; we shan't forget each other, shall we? You must make haste and grow a big girl, and then you can come and see me whenever you like. Oh! yes, you'll come back. Don't you know I'm a great conjuror, and I can see that you will?"

"When?" asked Anne, anxious and interested.

"Oh! in a few hundred days; say five hundred," he said boldly, in the certainty that she would have forgotten before the end of five.

"And then George won't send me back?"

He looked at her with undisguised admiration.

"No, Nancy; if I know anything at all, George won't be in any hurry to send you back then. Now, we mustn't keep Mr. Jones waiting any longer. Mind I don't say 'good-bye;' it is 'to our next merry meeting!'"

She tried to get up a smile, and allowed

him to put her in the carriage. George did not volunteer any farewell caress. Then the door was shut, and they drove off in the rain.

William Paton strolled to the end of the arched gateway for the small excitement of seeing the last of them. Looking round, he saw that George was watching too. When the chaise was finally out of sight, they turned back together.

"Thank Heaven!" exclaimed George, with much fervour if little devotion.

His father chuckled. He was in an aggravating mood; not that that was uncommon.

"All right, my lad," he said; "'it is always best to begin with a little aversion!'"

CHAPTER VII.

THE WHIRLIGIG OF TIME.

ANNE's reception at home was not particularly striking in any way. The fatted calf was a merely negative quantity; that is to say, she was not punished at all, nor scolded to any serious extent, and very likely this had been so far beyond her expectations that it gave something of a festive character to the occasion. Her father, after a really affectionate, though undemonstrative greeting, retired to entertain Mr. Jones in the dining-room. Her mother hugged her a good deal, and went the length of threatening to become hysterical. But Mrs. Stephens happened to be sitting with her at the time, having come on a mission of consolation, and she showed such energy in combating the symptoms that the child found herself pretty well forgotten, and felt small rather than interesting. She somehow effaced herself in a sidelong, hesitating retreat, and proceeded a story higher, where she found Henry Stephens performing the same work of mercy as his mother towards a really mournful looking Hester.

Here, indeed, she met with a certain amount of enthusiasm, and her spirits rose a little as she felt the delights of being a heroine. Henry allowed curiosity so far to smother his conscientious desire to improve the occasion as to listen with ill-disguised interest to the story of her adventures, though he would not desert his colours so far as to ask any questions, and from time to time would throw a sop to Cerberus, his conscience, in the form of a pious sigh. Little Hester clung to her sister and would not let her go; and when at last a special tea, long after hours, was brought in for her individual enjoyment, Anne began to think that a home-coming had its attractions. She did not go so far as to admit to herself that the tidy nursery, the cleanly meal, the general impression of firelight and well-ordered domesticity were intrinsically preferable to the hugger-mugger of Aunt Theresa's room at the Stag. But it certainly struck her as being less repellent than usual.

Probably this pleasant impression would not have lasted long. In fact, it had begun to wear off by the end of forty-eight hours; but before she had time to fret over much at the old yoke, the heavier for her experience of absolute emancipation, the day came for her to go to school. She had taken the sentence when it had been announced to her, with a calmness not unmingled with satisfaction, which considerably surprised Hester and somewhat chilled her. But, indeed, the outburst of affection between the sisters, on the first evening, had been merely phenomenal, and they had not been long in returning to their old terms of affectionate estrangement. But on the last day, Hester, who was always easily moved by a sentimental crisis, showed a tearful clinging devotion which ought to have touched Anne. Perhaps it failed of this effect, for on this occasion again, Anne found herself the heroine of the hour, a position she was quite capable of enjoying. As she was by no means heart-broken herself, it was rather pleasant to witness the emotion of her acquaintance. She went off cheerfully enough, clasping in one hand the favourite marble which Bob, her truest mourner, had pressed upon her in the hour of their surreptitious parting, and waving her handkerchief to the effective group of friends and kindred on the doorstep. The last she saw of them, Mrs. Stephens was offering Mrs. Paton a smelling-bottle, and the weeping Hester was being led back into the house between Henry and Mary Stephens, who were bending over her in attitudes of consolation.

So Anne entered on her school life, which ran its even course thenceforth, in the same seminary, till she was turned out, formed and finished, at eighteen. There is not much to relate about that period. Records of school-days are apt to fall flat on the general public above the age of sixteen. Apple-pie beds and bolster-fights, clandestine suppers of ginger-beer and jam-puffs; the grand passions inspired in and by the young gentlemen of Dr. Birchem's Academy over the way; the romantic friendships in which girls rehearse among themselves all the devotions, the unrequited attachments, the jealousies and lovers' quarrels of future years: at the time it was all very funny or very sad, sparkling comedy or heartbreaking tragedy. But even to ourselves the flavour soon goes, for it was youth only which gave it in the first place. The effervescence was the best part of the champagne—perhaps it was only gooseberry after all—and the effervescence is gone.

Taking it all round, it may be said that Anne enjoyed this period of her life. The restraint was little less than that of home, but there was congenial companionship, and that inestimable safety-valve freedom of discussion; it must be owned that, in liberty of speech, when alone with her contemporaries, Anne sufficiently distinguished herself. By the end of her time she had, as it were, outlived several generations of school-fellows, and had acquired a sort of prescriptive right to leadership. She did not avail herself of the privilege to any great extent, perhaps she could not do so. Her emotions, though not very lightly stirred, were strong; but her will was, if anything, weak. She made a tolerable leader in times of popular feeling, but she was no ruler and had no ambition to rule. Nor, though she liked to be liked, had she any morbid cravings for affection. She took her part in the incipient flirtations with the Birchemite youth, partly from an instinct of flirtation, but more because it was a recognized fashion. It did not absolutely bore her, but certainly it did not amuse, much less agitate her. In spite of occasional utterances of perversity to the contrary effect, she did not greatly care for boys; as associates among her contemporaries she preferred girls. With grown men it was different; from thirty upwards she was devoted to the sex, and had exerted her fascinations on every master in the establishment.

Perhaps this indifference to comparatively immature masculine homage helped to keep things pleasant for her in the school circle. Certainly she was, on the whole, popular with her school-fellows. She made no bosom friends, but she had no enemies; and there were plenty of girls with whom she was on such terms as to get an occasional invitation for the holidays. The least generous of them forgave her her marvellous and growing beauty for the sake of her want of interest in it. She was not unconscious of it and never pretended to be so; but she seemed to care little about it, and, though she would spend over an hour at her toilet on any special occasion, as a rule she was so careless of her personal appearance as barely to miss slovenliness. Her training had made this a practically impossible fault, but these combined instincts remained—an hereditary legacy from the many-headed monster, and not the only bequest of the kind either.

Among the ambitious of her little world she excited as little jealousy as among the frivolous. Her general mediocrity earned the pardon of her particular genius. She could not draw, she could not paint, though her feeling for colour was good; she could not even play as an ordinary show pupil should play, she had neither execution nor expression. All her reports ended in "moderate" or "fair," at best "a slight improvement;" only her singing-mistress and the little French dancing-master could not find words to express their feelings. Perhaps she did not actually dance better than many other girls, but there was a singular appropriateness, an expressiveness about her movements, her gestures, her whole deportment which made beholders forgive a certain unconventionality in these respects. But as for her singing! In the last months of her school career, at any rate, the maids would loiter cautiously on the stairs, if chance led them past the parlour at the time Miss Paton was having her singing-lesson; and when the windows stood open on summer afternoons, the distant tones of that voice would slacken or arrest the steps of the casual passer-by. Everybody knew this, but the envy it was calculated to excite was soothed when

Anne came down, good-humoured and cheerful, to make preposterous blunders over the use of the globes, or to sit down to the composition of the feeblest of essays, with the help of a pocket dictionary, for to the end of her days she never thoroughly learned to spell.

The girls themselves were glad enough to let her melt them into easy tears, when she would stand leaning against the trunk of the big walnut-tree, in the summer twilight, while they settled down around her on the grass like a flock of doves in their white gowns, listening to " Home, sweet home," sung with a pathos quite as instinctive, quite as conventional if you will, as that with which years before her untrained voice had rendered " Barbara Allen " in the coffee-room of the Stag Inn.

In point of fact, Anne was large-minded and altogether cosmopolitan in her ideas on the subject of home. The thought of it, though no longer repugnant, awakened no specially tender feeling in her breast. It amused her to make the girls cry, so she exerted every power of expression she possessed to that end ; if the chorus was choked in sobs she was triumphant. But she did not feel at all inclined to tears herself and rather wondered what they found to cry about. She was glad when the holidays came, and sorry when they ended ; perhaps, from the mere force of tradition and example, she imagined herself to be both more glad and more sorry than she really was, for Anne did not possess the domestic instinct.

It would have been quite possible for her to go home at last rather as a stranger, a visitor on terms of ordinary cordial politeness, than as a daughter returning to her only natural place, under her father's roof. If she had been at school at any considerable distance some such estrangement would probably have grown up, for school terms were not then the too brief respite from holidays which parents and guardians represent them as being now-a-days. But being so near home Anne had been saved from this. There was no relaxation of the rule against incidental holidays, but she was never out of touch of her kindred, and felt she was not. Hester, too, had been with her during her last year of school-life, and in all that regarded family feeling, as indeed in most other points, Hester was the exact antipodes of Anne. Forgetfulness, at least, was impossible, in the face of her constant references and reminiscences, and the elder sister was too good-natured to be otherwise than amusedly pleased at her cooing delight over a home-letter or the discovery of a common friend.

Therefore, when it was time for her to go home for good, Anne found it quite natural, and was content, not enthusiastic but content. Natural indeed it was. The Clapham to which she returned at eighteen was practically the same place she had known at eight. Births, deaths, and marriages there had been, of course, but there never seemed to be a vacancy anywhere. Among the deaths must be counted that of Joseph Stephens. A quiet, silent, somewhat ponderous boy, he had faded gently out of life, at about the age of fourteen, much as his father had done before him. He had been loved, poor Joseph ; he was mourned, sincerely mourned ; and he was forgotten. It had been so easy to forget him, even when he was alive and in the same room with the rest of the family ; a modest impersonality, whose final obliteration made no more sensible gap in the home circle than does the subsidence of a wave, that never comes to breaking, upon the surface of the ocean. Though the Stephenses were still their next-door neighbours, Anne had not seen much of any of them during the years of her school-life; of Henry least of all. They had always been in the habit of spending Christmas with the head of the house of Barling— Mrs. Stephens had been Maria Barling— and Henry's summer holidays did not coincide with those of his little friend. That was how their fond parents spoke to one another of Henry and Anne respectively. When the adjective became manifestly absurd it was changed to "young," but no further alteration had been made by the time Anne came home.

Henry Stephens was plain Henry still. Sir Robert clung to life with the tenacity of many weakly persons, and seemed almost

to get stronger in his old age. If the
thought that this conduct was inconsiderate
ever did occur to his great nephew, Henry
never gave it utterance, even to himself,
waiting with a decorous patience which
disclaimed all idea of waiting. Yet there
were times when the situation caused him
a certain amount of perplexity, just enough
to make him respectfully plaintive with
Providence. The position of heir-apparent
is not altogether an easy one. Henry
was now nearly three-and-twenty. He
had just concluded a blameless career at
college. There he had made few friends
and no enemies, and had worked with a
steady diligence which seemed to merit
a higher reward than the respectable, but
not striking academical honours which
were all he actually achieved. Most of
his contemporaries had already started on
what was to be the career of their lives,

while he still hung, like Mahomet's coffin, between the earth of sordid money-making and the heaven of landed proprietorship. He had been idle at home for some months on the strength of a slight paralytic seizure of Sir Robert's; but the last accounts had reported a surprising rally, and this indefinite idleness did not at all suit the actual condition of the family finances. He was a good deal exercised on the subject.

"I cannot but feel," he said, "that there are circumstances in my case which place unusual difficulties in the choice of a profession."

"That's true," sighed Mrs. Stephens. "Of course a profession it must be; you could not go into business. No, not a word, Henry; I know what you are going to say, you are going to allude to the expense." (Henry had not thought of it.)

"But you only pain me. Do you think I grudge anything to keep you in the position to which you are entitled? And indeed we can afford it now. Dear Mary, as one may say, provided for; Jack at sea; and your uncle Barling has pledged himself to keep up his interest in Jim, so long as he deserves it."

"Indeed, I have no wish to go into business. I had not thought of it."

"I knew my own boy would agree with me," said Mrs. Stephens with sublime contentment. "And you wouldn't be a doctor. My dear, promise me never to think of being a doctor. It is not a profession for one of your expectations; in my young days it was scarcely considered a profession at all. I couldn't bear to think of you driving about the country lanes in a one-horse trap, rolling pills, with a red lamp over the surgery door. And if you should grow red whiskers! so many of them do, and I think that is why I have such a horror of red-haired men, from association you know, because of young Dr. Higgins who used to draw my teeth when I was a little girl. He was a vulgar young man, and untruthful I am sorry to say, always used to tell me it wouldn't hurt, and he had red whiskers. It would make me very unhappy to think of you like that."

"*I* have a great respect for the medical profession," said Henry, with the suavest, most respectful suggestion of reproof; "but I do not myself wish to be a doctor. For the navy I am too old, for the army I have neither the means nor the inclination. Were I to follow the natural bent of my inclination I should enter the church."

"The very thing, my dear! It is a

most gentlemanly profession, I'm sure;
one which could never stand in your light
in any turn of events. And with your
uncle Barling's interest—Really I do not
see that you can do better."

"I should be ungrateful indeed to doubt
my dear uncle's generosity, after the many
unmerited proofs of it which he has given
me for years past," said Henry, with
feeling. "Yet there is a certain irre-
vocability about the clerical profession
which is deterrent to me, in the unassured
condition of my prospects. Indeed, I
cannot but foreshadow to myself occasions,
when the double character of minister and
lord of the manor might become embarrassing."

"The Reverend Sir Henry Stephens.
It sounds very well, my dear."

"In the matter of euphony it is
unexceptionable, as you say. Perhaps,

indeed, my objections are unreasonably sentimental, but, such as they are, to me they are insuperable." He paused a moment, to let her feel the force of his determination. She did not well know what insuperable meant, perhaps, but his tone so clearly meant " I won't," that she gave up the pleasing vision with a sigh ; and with a smile of respectful approbation he went on—" The power of ideas in the world, dear mother, can scarcely be overestimated, and sentiment, in its influence on the actions of mankind, is a factor of such importance that it cannot be eliminated without detriment to the correctness of the calculation."

It will be judged from this speech that Henry's early fondness for Johnsonian diction, combined with admirable views, had not diminished as he grew up. He did not always talk like this—not quite always. But on the slightest opening for a moral essay he could never resist the temptation. For this reason he and Captain Paton, though in feeling and theory the best of friends, did not greatly affect one another's society. Their styles killed each other, and in the interests of art they felt they were better apart.

"For instance," continued Henry, being now in the vein and encouraged by his mother's admiring attention : "to take the most typical of all sentiments, that which the world is pleased to consider as the passion *par excellence*, I allude to the emotion of love. How, from the earliest ages, has this sentiment, especially when complicated by a sensibility to physical beauty, shaken half a world to its centre. I have read somewhere a striking remark bearing on this subject." (He had found it, as an anonymous quotation, in an old

"Gentleman's Pocket Book," where—scissors and paste making authors acquainted with strange bedfellows—it had appeared between a couplet of Byron and a recipe for milk punch; and it might have been by the man in the moon, for all he knew, as he certainly had never troubled the original). "'If' says this ingenious author, 'the nose of Cleopatra had been shorter, the face of the world would have been changed.' The same might be said of—Mother! oh, good gracious, look quick; who, who is that?"

This conversation had taken place as the mother and son were strolling back from the afternoon constitutional which they took with praiseworthy regularity. They were within sight of their own gate when the carriage which had attracted Henry's attention rolled past them. Before Mrs. Stephens could collect her senses enough to see or to understand the cause of his unwonted excitement, the carriage had drawn up a little further on, and two young ladies sprang out. One at once pushed open a garden gate, and ran lightly up the path, but the taller of the two lingered.

A great horse-chestnut tree grew near the gate, a tree now all covered with the waxen flower-tapers which are its votive offerings at the shrine of summer, and the girl, standing on tip-toe, was struggling with one great pile of blossom, which she was trying to pick. She had bent the bough down to her with difficulty, and was just breaking off her prize in triumph, when the branch slipped from her grasp and sprang back, getting entangled in her bonnet and hair. She caught the bough again in both hands, with a little cry of amused dismay, and so stood helpless, but the next moment some one had seized it and she was free to disengage herself. This she did by simply untying the strings and letting the bonnet go; her hair she shook free with an impatience which released it, indeed, but sent all flowing, a sudden shower of sunshine, about her face. Whereupon she tossed it out and laughed. There she stood, a saucy dryad, creamy blossoms dropped upon her green gown and tangled in her golden hair, her eyes dancing with laughter; and there stood Henry, the bonnet dangling in his hand and all his eloquence put to flight.

"Thanks," she said. Then her blue eyes opened wider. "Why! it—it is Henry Stephens!" The laughter from her eyes seemed to overflow and ripple softly into silver sound. "Don't you know me, Henry?" she said. "I'm Anne."

CHAPTER VIII.

BRINGS ABOUT ITS REVENGES.

PERHAPS the fact had dawned upon Henry's dazzled consciousness even before Anne declared herself. Still he found nothing more brilliant to say than that the pleasure had been so entirely unexpected that— that—in fact—when the arrival on the scene of Captain and Mrs. Paton, followed by Hester, relieved his embarrassment.

Mrs. Paton, a little taken aback at first by Anne's dishevelled appearance, yet, in her mother's heart, blessed her with rejoicing for her beauty, and kissed her the more tenderly if that could be. The impression made on the Captain was much less ecstatic; nevertheless, with a really magnanimous effort, he suppressed all rebuke and even comment, and Anne acknowledged the magnanimity with a pang of something like remorse. She had come back with such excellent resolutions of submission; so careful she had meant to be of all the little fetishes and respectabilities of home; and, before she had even crossed the threshold, the vagabondage latent in her nature had broken out. Here she was, bareheaded, gloveless, with wild hair, talking confidentially in the open road to a young man, who was holding her bonnet, and whom she had hailed with silvery clearness by his Christian name. She felt touched by the paternal forbearance; it really seemed to represent a high ideal of fatherly affection. She coloured as she had not done for Henry, and dropped her eyes, looking the more divine. There was something touching in the serious, detailed resolutions of mutual forbearance made to their own souls by this father and daughter; the very painful minuteness of the care, the heroism of the effort, only assured its hopelessness.

By the time the first introductions and family greetings were over, Mrs. Stephens had come up. She kissed Anne affectionately (by this time they were in the domestic sanctity of the garden), and looked at Henry inexpressibly. But Henry was looking at Anne.

"I was just asking your son, dear madam, if he would be able and willing to give us the pleasure of his company to-morrow evening. Is it too much to hope that you will come too?"

In all the fifteen years of their acquaintance, Captain Paton had never issued an invitation in less ceremonious terms than these. Later in the day a note would follow; it was a propriety never omitted.

"Just a few friends, dear Maria, to celebrate dear Anne and dear Hester's return. It seems like old days, doesn't it, to see all the dear children together again?"

"Scarcely children now, Jane; and, my love, if you will excuse the hint, I think you will do well to bear that fact in mind."

Henry was not scorched by the maternal glare which accompanied the hint, and Jane Paton misunderstood it. She raised her weak faint blue eyes with a puzzled expression.

"You think this cap is too young looking? But I have ordered another for tomorrow. What have I ever done, Maria," she said plaintively, "that you should think me a mother to put myself in rivalry with my own daughters?"

Mrs. Stephens looked at Anne, on in front, the resplendent substance of the wan shadow her mother. She did not smile, for she had absolutely no sense of humour, but because she was good-natured her heart smote her.

"I was not thinking of your cap, or of anything of the kind," she said; then added hastily, "What a sweet-looking girl dear Hester has grown into!"

"And Anne?" asked the mother anxiously. "She is untidy now, of course, but I do think she is improved."

"My dear Jane," said dear Maria, bracingly, to say the least, "why on earth should you treat *me* to false modesty nowadays? Of course we all know that Anne is a beauty."

"Do you think so?" said Mrs. Paton, with an expression her friend mentally stigmatized as an affected simper, so aggravating to her that she could scarcely refrain from a snap.

It did not please her to find Henry entirely agreeing in her own expressed opinion of Anne's looks. When, at tea-time—the Stephenses still dined early—his sister Mary asked him whether he had found Anne as pretty as she herself had always thought her:

"Your misapplication of words is absurd," he said. "A doll is pretty; a daisy is pretty."

"Dear me!" cried Mary, cheerfully. "Then if Anne isn't pretty, what is she?"

"If," said Henry, deliberately, "I were obliged to qualify Miss Paton by any epithet I should venture to say she is radiant."

"Miss Paton!" repeated Jim, irreverently. "Oh, my!"

And the twins giggled, and then pretended they were choking, and were told sharply that, of the two, perhaps that was the more entirely unladylike habit.

"Well," said Mary, perhaps hoping to slip in the remark under cover of this rebuke, "I always did think you were a real Christian, you know, and now you have got so far as to meet one of the shining ones——"

"Are you aware what you are saying, Mary?" said Mrs. Stephens, snappishly. "I know you don't study your 'Pilgrim's Progress' with much attention, or in a very proper spirit; still I think you might be sensible of the profanity of comparing Anne Paton to an angel."

"Isn't she an angel, Henry?" asked Jim.

"'A creature,'" quoted Henry with a sort of solemn melody (he was rather great at recitations of a serious kind), "'a creature not too bright and good for human nature's daily food.'"

"No," murmured Mary, acquiescently; "not at all. I suspect not, at any rate."

Mrs. Stephens regretted the effect their young friend's arrival had already had on the tone of her family, and begged that the discussion might be dropped; and dropped it was. Only after this night Mary always used to inquire privately for Anne as "the shining one"; and, in spite of the profanity as well as of the incongruity of the comparison, to which he could not long be blind, Henry somehow liked the nickname, and would let it pass without rebuke.

It may be guessed from these facts that a change had passed over Mary herself;

she was, in fact, nearly emancipated. For some months past she had been engaged to a thoroughly eligible young stock-broker, of a wealthy stock-broking family; they were to be married as soon as the house her father-in-law elect was building for the young couple should be ready for them. The engagement, so eminently satisfactory, gave her a certain tone of independence; it gave her a standing, even put her somewhat into the position of a benefactress to her family. She was too generous to presume upon this, but the consciousness of it was invigorating, and there were times, now, when she could detach herself from the neutral-tinted Stephens background by some happy touch of individuality.

The next evening the Stephenses came in a little late. Mrs. Stephens, who, privately, liked to drain the cup of every entertainment from the brim to the dregs, had been obliged to yield to Henry's sense of fitness, to come fashionably late, and to promise to retire respectfully early. Notwithstanding, when they arrived, they found the gathering had not yet progressed beyond the circular stage; all the guests were seated round the room, conversing in subdued tones with their next neighbours. It did not look festive, but this was the recognized first stage at a party. Nor, in general, did the company look exuberantly lively; a solemn cheerfulness pervaded the scene, a sort of autumnal serenity seemed to beam mildly from many benignant matrons and elderly gentlemen. By degrees, Henry made out that there was a youthful element in the room, but, with the one exception of the daughter of the house, it was too well-bred to come to the fore; it diffused merely a subdued, surreptitious vivacity, such a half melancholy breath of spring as lurks in the perfume of autumn violets. Decidedly the occasion was more or less serious. Henry did not mind this himself; he shone chiefly on serious occasions. But Mary, after the first glance, experienced an awful desire to laugh; she was not yet so far unshackled as not to feel the inclination a little profane.

Mrs. Paton came to meet them. Ten years before she had been still an elegant woman, willowy and colourless yet not without a certain slim grace. But time had not dealt kindly with her. She was now undeniably thin and reedy, colossally lank; she looked washed out, too, and fairly bleached. She had never had much taste in dress, but to-night, in addition to the truly depressing cap which was to mark her sense of approaching age, she had arrayed herself in palest straw-colour silk ; it seemed to accentuate her dimness ; with her parchment-like pallor, her faded hair, her strangely over-grown look, she somehow suggested images of a gigantic sea-kale. Mrs. Stephens, in bugles—for the general impression she made was always rather of bugles than black—looked healthy and invigorating beside her; a trifling exuberance of form and colour, such as the years had brought to her, seemed a fault on the right side when she was placed over against her friend.

"You are late," said the hostess; "you know, Maria, we never feel our little gatherings complete till you have come. None of us do."

She added that with a kind of spasm of remembrance. Her eyes sought Anne, and Mrs. Stephens' going the same way, saw Henry already beside her. Anne was standing, she very seldom sat; and

Mrs. Stephens' first impression was that she was not anything so wonderful to look at after all. In fact, she was dressed to a character, and the character did not suit. Hester, coming forward with her sweet shy smile to greet Henry's mother, of whom she was sincerely fond, was in perfect keeping with the implied conception. With the soft plain braids of her nut-brown hair, hair smooth as satin by nature, in her simple white muslin and blue ribbons, exquisitely fresh and neat from head to foot, she looked a perfect type of youth and goodness; her whole being lent itself to the situation. All Anne's rebelled. It had not been a practical rebellion; she was far too indifferent to dress, so far as it affected her looks, even to desire a protest against any arrangement made for her. But every curl of her hair, every line of her figure, every flash and sparkle of her eye, seemed to call attention to the infelicitous idea of making Anne Paton represent that particular type. The effect was not to make her insipid; that was an impossibility. But it gave her a certain inappropriate, half-reclaimed appearance, which did not show her off to advantage.

"I am afraid you have forgotten the lessons of your childhood, Henry," she said; "I remember you used to be such a punctual boy. But you are very late, for you."

"If I could have dared to hope that the time would have seemed long to you," simpered Henry.

"Oh! it hasn't particularly."

"I cannot say the same," said Henry, with a graceful suggestion of a suppressed sigh. "The last twenty-four hours have seemed very long to me, Miss Paton."

Anne opened her eyes upon him for a

moment to their fullest extent, then broke into one of her irrepressible fits of laughter.

"Are you staying in Clapham, now?" she asked abruptly. "Oh! I hope you are going to stay."

There was a genuine earnestness about her tone, which sent a serious thrill of ecstasy through every fibre of the deluded Henry's being.

"Until I have decided upon my future career there is nothing to call me to any other spot. That decision is a serious one; I shall presume to hope for your interest, perhaps for your guidance, in the matter."

"Oh, my guidance is of no use to any body. But I shall like to hear about it all the same; your ideas are almost sure to do me good. How do you always find just the right words to express your feelings in?" said Anne, with the reverent curiosity of a young and ardent disciple thirsting for information.

"When the heart is moved the tongue is taught," said Henry, and felt that was rather neat.

But Anne shook her head.

"I don't think that is always the case. But you must come and see me often, like you used to do, and tell me what you mean."

Truth compels the statement that she was not looking at Henry as she uttered this audacious invitation. Her sweet, appealing eyes were engaged in focussing Mrs. Stephens, who, free at last from dear Jane's moral button-holing, was bearing down upon them, and had just got within hearing distance, as Anne spoke. In that instant's interchange of glances the gage was thrown down and taken up between the woman and the girl, and Anne's inmost heart leaped with the joy of battle.

"I am sorry to interrupt your first talk with our little Anne," said Mrs. Stephens, sweetly; "but Miss St. Clare positively won't begin to play unless you can turn over for her. She says she is so accustomed to having you she cannot trust any one else. These geniuses," she beamed to Anne, "you know, they must be humoured."

"Miss St. Clare," said Henry, with suppressed fury, for Anne was looking at him curiously, "must be labouring under some singular misconception. I may have assisted at her performances twice, perhaps."

"Never mind, Henry; go now," said Anne. And in her tone was such a mixture of sympathy, authority, entreaty and mutual understanding, that the victim went off smiling to the sacrifice, while Mrs. Stephens began to lose her temper, and therewith her last faint chance of victory. Not that Anne's next remark showed anything of a victor's insolence; on the contrary, her manner became childlike and bland to a bewildering degree.

"I am so glad I never have to trouble anybody to turn over for me," she said; "I am sure they must find it such a nuisance. But you see I don't play, worth speaking of."

"Oh! you mustn't be shy," said Mrs. Stephens, with a sudden increase of cordiality. "Perhaps you don't practise enough. Susan and Sarah both practise for three hours a day.

"How nice that must be!" admiringly. "I suppose they generally play duets? No, I never practise if I can help it, and I always get Hester to play my accompaniments."

"Oh! you sing?"

"A little," murmured Anne.

"That will be a treat for Henry," put in Mary, finding the temptation irresistible. "He loves nothing so much as singing."

"I hope he didn't lose his voice when it changed. I remember quite well the little hymns we used to sing together, before I went to school."

"You seem to have a good memory," said Mrs. Stephens. It was a rash invitation to a finishing thrust, but she was beyond fighting scientifically.

"I never forget," said Anne, gravely. "I remember even the names and words of a good many of them. There was one in particular—'Oh! that will be joyful,' I think. Am I right? The one with a chorus about 'meet to part no more.' I always was fond of that one."

Mrs. Stephens suddenly saw a friend at the opposite corner of the room, and was *obliged* to run away.

"Anne!" remonstrated Mary, fanning her flushed cheeks. "You are every bit as naughty as you used to be."

To her surprise, Anne answered with a little sigh, impatient rather than penitent.

"I know," she said; "and yet I did think I should be good to-night. I always feel I ought to be when I have on this gown. I keep my most 'good' songs to go with it."

"What do you mean?"

"Why, I always feel like what I am dressed in. Don't you?"

"No; I don't think so," said Mary, reflectively. Her blue gown simply represented the fact that her Frank liked to see her in blue.

"I suppose, then, you don't care for dressing up? I love it! But it got me into the most terrible scrape at school only a little while ago. You won't tell anybody? I went down on my knees to Miss Robinson to beg her not to let them know at home;—I wouldn't get up till she promised. They must never even guess it."

Of course Mary promised. Miss St. Clare was in the thick of that bloody engagement, the Battle of Prague; and, under cover of the rattle of musketry and the groans of the dying, Anne told her tale.

"I was just learning 'Voi che sapete,' and it struck me that I should get on so much better if I were to practise it in character."

"'Voyky ——' What's that?"

"It is Italian: 'Voi che sapete che cosa e l'amor."

"Do you know Italian?" said Mary, somewhat impressed.

"Not a word—that's the beauty of it!

Don't you see?—if I had, I should never have been allowed to learn that song. But they thought, as I didn't understand, it couldn't matter."

"Why? Was it wicked?"

"No; only it is all about love. They appear to think that wicked; it only seems silly to me. But I wasn't going to learn a song that I didn't know the meaning of. How could I ever sing it right? It was absurd!

"How could you find out?"

"There was an Italian master, who comes for some of the girls—such a dear! He would do anything for me. They all would do that; but this one I loved best of any of them almost. Mary, I think the thing I should like best in the world would be to go to Italy. Don't you like Italians?"

"They are papists," said Mary, doubtfully.

"But that is rather interesting. I mean," Anne added hastily, "of course it would be wicked for us, but in them it seems different, somehow. Well, I got Signor Barberini to translate it to me—tell me all about the story, and who sang this song. I found out it was a page."

"A page?"

"Yes. So, after that, I spent weeks making the dress—secretly. I copied it out of one of the pictures in Mrs. Markham's 'History of France:' everything, down to the shoes and—and those long, long stockings, you know," said Anne, between laughing and blushing. "At last, one Saturday afternoon, when every one was out of the way, I put it on. There was no one to see me, Mary, and I had locked the door. Then I got into a right sort of position, and began to sing. You can't think how I sang that time! I never sang like it, before or since."

"Well, did she catch you?"

"It was worse than that! Just as I was beginning the second verse, I heard somebody take it up—somebody in the street. It was a man's voice; not right for that song, but oh! Mary, it was lovely—more than lovely! I forgot all about my dress and everything. The front windows have little iron balconies to them there. The window was open—I had forgotten that when I began to sing. I rushed out on to the balcony, in that dress, to look at the voice, and—— Mary, it was George!"

"I don't know whom you mean," said Mary, faintly. She was beginning to find these revelations a trifle too Bohemian.

"My cousin, George Paton. I knew him at once; he has not changed a bit. Besides, I had seen their names—his and Uncle Will's—up on the posters, to perform at Richmond that week, so I was prepared to see either of them about. But he didn't know me, I'm sure," she added hastily. "And just then, oh! Miss Robinson drove up to the gate with Lady Mary, Louisa Ponsonby's mamma, and saw George staring up at the window as if the house were haunted. Of course they looked too, —I was too frightened to move—and Miss Robinson got quite yellow; but Lady Mary shouted! They were always scolding Louisa for the way she laughs; they said it was vulgar—but it is just like Lady Mary's, and they never called that vulgar. I've heard Miss Robinson say herself, 'I do like to hear your dear mother laugh; there is something so genuine about it, so—so spontaneous!' I'm sure Louisa's was spontaneous enough; at any rate, half the times none of us could make out what she was laughing about, and I don't believe she knew herself."

"Well, but what happened? What was the end?"

"That was the end—that laugh. I really don't know any more. I never felt so dreadful in all my life. Only," she added after a pause, "I knew for certain that I could sing 'Voi che sapete;' I saw it in George's face that one moment before he caught sight of me." And, though she was now covered with very permissible blushes at the mere relation of her escapade, it was evident that this was an abiding, even a superabundant consolation.

Mary sat and reflected for a few moments. Then she said—

" Sing that to-night.'

"No; to-night I am going to sing 'Home, sweet home,' they will like that." With Anne, "they" always meant her parents. "Don't talk to me any more," she added suddenly; "I expect I shall have to begin in a few minutes, and I want to think myself into it. I mean to sing it really well."

Quite undisturbed by Mary's bewildered stare, she put her hands together, composed herself, and, with the rapidity of a conjuring trick, entered into a state of profound *recueillement*. By the time Henry came up, beaming and hopeful, for his expected reward, she was ready. Her very voice was different; there was no trace of teasing or coquetry in the gentle tones in which she repeated the explanation offered before to Mrs. Stephens, quietly rejecting his assistance. And when she went to stand by the piano, at which Hester was already seated, it would have been hard to say which of the two looked the more perfectly domesticated!

During the few opening bars she stood with her hands clasped loosely in front of her, her eyes bent on the ground; then, with a sort of slow flash, she raised them, seemed to gather in the sentiment of home with one luminous glance, which, finally, rested on her mother. She sang till her own eyes were positively filled with tears; then, as the last notes died away, she slid through the storm of applause and congratulation, with that same smiling, tearful look, and sinking down before her mother, who was furtively wiping her eyes in a distant corner, she took up one of the long, feeble-looking hands, and kissed it. Then she recovered herself, jumped up, and laughed a little, softly.

Was it at the world? at herself? She had no idea. The extraordinary double consciousness, which made her very insincerity sincere, enabled her to laugh, with one half of her being, at the other half, even while that was still tremulous with passion or emotion—deliberately evoked at first, then as deliberately surrendered to.

If her voice had excited admiration, her tableau occasioned an amount of edification which would have amused her. Her reputation as a reformed character, a model daughter, was established for the nonce; happily, it occurred to no one to imagine that she might be a finished actress. The company then present, whose idea of histrionic art was a compound of the Beggar's Opera and a ranting Hamlet in a barn, really did not know enough of the drama to perceive that the action or expression was dramatic. It was too like nature to be art; art, in their opinion, being artistic in proportion to its unlikeness to anything on earth.

Perhaps only Mrs. Stephens was dubious, and she kept her doubts, for the present, to herself. Anne, who had really sung herself into one of her transient fits of virtue, was irreproachable all the rest of the evening. To Henry she was sisterly and unaffected; but she made no further attempts to monopolize him. She was working diligently round the company; talking to shy girls, with the prattling naïveté of a newly-emancipated school-miss; avoiding their brothers; listening to all the old ladies and gentlemen, with a sympathetic grace which it is not given to all to assume.

Nevertheless, in the maternal confidence of her chamber, Mrs. Stephens thus summed up the moral lessons of the evening.

"Well, if this is what comes of your fine boarding-school education, I am truly thankful that no daughter of mine has ever left my roof! A humble roof it may be, but, under it, my precious girls have the advantage of a mother's eye, a mother's watchful care; and as I look round upon them, I can say, with a thankful heart, that there is not one but is growing up to be a blessing to her mother now, and to her husband by-and-bye. And what are all the airs and graces, and shakes and trills, ever taught by some poor benighted papist for his daily bread, to such qualites as that? And so have I said to Jane Paton, scores of times; and I pray that she may not live to say I was a true prophet," she concluded, with oracular and impressive incoherence.

"I thought," said Mary, "you were rather anxious at one time to send Sue and Sally to boarding-school?"

"Yes, I was; and remember it, my dear, as an example of the short-sightedness of our poor weak nature. To-day you see me thankful—thankful on my knees, that a want of means, against which I foolishly rebelled, prevented me from sending those two innocent babes to receive a training more fitted to turn out a—a—an opera-singer than anything else."

"Mamma, pray don't say anything about opera-singers to Henry!"

"Mary, I must beg you to leave off these foolish jokes."

"I didn't mean it for a joke."

"Then I am sorry to think you have such a poor opinion of your brother. I am surprised at you. Henry is a young man of sterling principles, and excellent expectations, and for both reasons is scarcely likely to stake the happiness of his future on a little affected minx, who positively throws herself at his head."

"Do you think Anne Paton is that, mamma?"

"I name no names," said Mrs. Stephens, with a sniff.

CHAPTER IX.

AFTER THE CONQUEST.

ANNE had been little more than a week at home before she discovered, first, that Henry was in love with her, and—for him—very much in love; secondly, that, for reasons into which she did not trouble to inquire, Mrs. Stephens was exceedingly annoyed at his attentions to her. Henry's devotion might have affected her but little, had not his mother's opposition acted as a stimulus. Had Mrs. Stephens but known it, she, and she alone, was the cause that Anne even tolerated her admirer. Left to herself she would scarcely have done even this; roused by opposition, for a time she almost led him on.

But as for Captain and Mrs. Paton, so soon as their eyes were opened to the situation, Anne's reputation with them went up with a bound. All at once she found herself in the novel position of the good child of the household. In every way, short of words, she was made to feel that she had deserved well of her family, and that they were not ungrateful. At first this state of affairs was so new that it amused her; but by the end of a month or so she grew very weary of it.

And if her reputation became wearisome, so, far more, did Henry. She had rung all the changes on him; she knew all his little ways. She had flattered him, and he had swallowed every bait; she had snubbed him, and he had subsided without a murmur. She had posed as a disciple, and had found his eloquence only increased and exalted by love ; finally, she had done her very best to scandalize him, and had realized, with secret rage, why it is that love is painted blind.

At last one day, to her infinite relief, he informed her that he was shortly leaving Clapham for London. After a lengthy balancing of pros and cons, he had settled to begin to read for the bar. Certainly, viewed as an immediately, or even prospectively, remunerative profession, this left something to be desired ; in fact, the direct result of the move was a heavy call on the family purse. But no one who knew Henry or his mother would have doubted of the end of the debate. The practical question was indeed purely, even pressingly, financial ; the sentimental question was social ; and if they were incapable of receiving a simultaneous answer, there could be no hesitation as to which should have the preference.

On the day preceding his departure Anne was in the garden picking raspberries, and humming "Cherry Ripe" thereto, when she saw Henry coming down the path. By this time she had got so desperately tired of him that his approach was usually the signal for her departure; and Henry thought this a good sign. But to-day she wanted to finish her fruit-picking; she reflected also that his time was getting very short, and, in that belief, prepared to receive him cordially. She offered him some raspberries; he accepted them with a mysterious solemnity, eating them impressively, as though he were drinking a pledge. They strolled down to the end of the garden together; Henry seemed nervous, and his nervousness affected Anne in spite of herself. Across the corner of the walls was a board, once a stand for bee-hives, and on this they seated themselves.

"I have come to say good-bye, Anne," said Henry, solemnly; then, after a pause, "May I call you Anne?"

"Why not?" she said a little sharply, to hide some failing of heart. "You always do."

And, in fact, after the first day or two, he had fallen into the way of it again.

"But—if I have permission to do so still, it will be with, may I say a higher? I cannot say a sweeter, significance."

Again he paused, but Anne did not reply.

"I have just come from an interview with your parents. It was very gratifying to me to perceive that their sympathetic instincts had already partly divined what I had to say. They gave me their permission to address you; will you give me your own?"

Anne looked up stormily.

"If you have settled it all with them beforehand, I don't know what more you want."

"How can it be settled?" he said, deprecatingly. "Without your consent that of your parents can only legally justify me; morally, as a man and a gentleman, I should be indeed unjustifiable in forcing upon you a distasteful suit."

"Then," said Anne, rising, "that is finished."

"How so?"

"Because what you mention would be exceedingly distasteful to me."

Henry's face fell.

"Am I to understand that you refuse to allow me even to plead my cause?"

Anne was inexperienced, good-natured, above all profoundly indifferent.

"Oh! plead it if you like," she said

cheerfully. "A speech is always practice, isn't it? I don't want to be unkind, I'm sure; only let this be the last."

Was it his good or his evil genius that, for once in his life, prompted Henry to do the right thing?

"I have no speech to make," he said with a certain dignity; "only this: I love you."

Now Anne had not expected this. She had fully believed that he would have come primed with a tolerably lengthy, cut-and-dried discourse, unimpeachable in sentiment, faultless in expression, of which, once he had delivered his soul, he would be able to go upon his way, if not rejoicing, at least satisfied. And behold! he had so expressed himself as to leave no opening for mockery, for subterfuge, for anything but explicit declaration or flight. She was disconcerted, and could not conceal it.

"That is all; I fear you do not understand how much it is, to me at least. It is little enough to you, I suppose."

It was—very little; but how could she say so? She was too young to be deliberately cruel, though she could be so on impulse. Therefore, in the shame and fury of defeat, she began to cry. It was the worst thing she could have done; she knew it, and the knowledge made her cry worse—weep till all power of speech was gone. Now it was always very hard to bring home to Henry a sense of defeat. Moreover, with the singular infatuation of men who know women, if at all, exclusively from books, he was under the firm impression that a girl's "No," in such cases, was merely a conventional introduction to "Yes." Therefore he gathered not so much hope, which he had not lost, as courage from Anne's tears, and ventured on the next conventional move. He dropped on one knee before her, seized her unresisting hand and kissed it fervently. And as the fates would have it, suddenly upon this group came Hester. Neither of them had heard her light footstep upon the garden walk.

"Anne, Anne!" she cried, as she turned the corner; "father wants—Oh!!"

She stood transfixed. But Anne, crimson, panting, dishevelled, fled like a flash up the path and vanished into the house. Henry, looking, as he could not but look, a little foolish but not ill-satisfied, stood where he was and, after all, it was Hester who made the first move.

"Is it so?" she said, coming up to him with outstretched hands. "Oh! I am so glad, so glad!"

And then she too turned, and disappeared after Anne. Henry was left to get himself off the scene as he might, and, without knowing it, experienced something of the feeling of an actor when the curtain refuses to fall on a situation. He could not bring himself to go back through the house; he went out, through a door in the wall, into what had been a lane when Anne rushed along it to liberty years before. Now it was a road, between garden walls, for houses had sprung up in the fields of former days. He walked along for some time reflecting, partly with satisfaction, partly with a certain perplexity as to what his position really was. On the whole, he felt what would have been triumph in a man of stronger emotions. With Henry, it scarcely attained to this; he was not devoid of feelings, but they were all rounded off and muffled, never salient or distinct. He sincerely believed himself in love with Anne; but, in truth, he was only infatuated with her. There was nothing about her that his mind or even his heart recognized as really desirable, and yet he, not ardently, but earnestly desired her. She had bewitched him, so far she ruled him; yet even so there was no passion in the affair, nor ever could be.

Meanwhile the fate about which he was uncertain was being decided. When Hester had flown into the house, it had been with the intention of seeking Anne; but her mother waylaid her in the hall, fluttered and anxious for news. She had heard Anne's entrance, but had not dared to attack her on the subject: now the two women enjoyed nearly half an hour of perfect bliss in mutual confidences and speculations. At the end of that time Captain Paton entered and bade Hester call her sister.

Anne had long since recovered both from her tears and her agitation; and had begun to reflect on the difficulties of her situation. But serious as the scrape seemed, she could not, strange to say, summon up any other feeling than one of amusement. With the levity of youth, of natural disposition, of an untouched heart, she recalled the episode with a sense of something irresistibly funny; now and again, as she pictured the climax, she went off, all by herself and for the pure comedy of the thing, into stifled peals of laughter. She forgave Henry hours of boredom for the sake of the present mirth. One thing only she regretted, with a quaint, unformulated regret: that she could not have been in the body and out of the body at one and the same moment, so as to see the tableau as Hester must have seen it. This extraordinary desire to see her one self with the bodily eyes of her other self was rather often present to Anne in this still undeveloped, badly dove-tailed period of her life.

At Hester's summons she did begin to get a little nervous; she felt that if, now, she did not brace herself to hold her own, the whole morning's work might be wasted. And she was always rather afraid of her father, with a fear which had not enough of veneration in it to result in only deeper love. Yet even so the excitement was pleasant. Anne really delighted in sensations; even disagreeable ones she preferred to none. It was a pleasure to her, whenever her infant passions, of whatever kind, seemed to feel their legs; she liked to quiver with their struggles to escape. The mere knowledge that they existed, a knowledge often dormant for months at a time, had a sort of charm for her.

Captain Paton was sitting in his study chair before his writing-table; in the background Mrs. Paton was hovering indefinitely, like a benevolent spiritualistic manifestation.

"Sit down, my daughter," he began. And Anne sat down on the edge of a chair, wondering what, and how much, he knew. Mrs. Paton floated up and kissed her.

"Don't frighten her, Captain," she said. "Hester tells me the dear child has been quite upset. She is very young—younger than I could have wished to have experiences of this kind. Yes, Anne"—lifting a hand of playful reproof—"at your age I should never have thought of such things. Should I, Captain? Now, don't be flurried, darling"—with another kiss. "I'm here. I shall understand all about it."

Anne, thus encouraged, felt a choking, hysterical desire to laugh. The longing for the relief, the horrible anticipations of the result, brought tears to her eyes, and this absurdity made her want to laugh the more. Nobody ever imagined that Anne was a nervous girl; she would have been furious with any one who should have suggested the idea. But then nobody knew the extent to which she possessed the artist temperament. She herself, as yet, was only feeling at this fact in the dark, catching glimpses of the truth with a flash which rather bewildered than revealed.

"A little emotion," said the Captain, condescendingly, "is natural, and not unseemly, under the circumstances. But the heart, though it may claim a temporary remission, cannot altogether exempt us from the necessity of attending to mere worldly affairs; and it is from a practical, a business point of view, that I have to speak to Anne now. No doubt"—he smiled in a way which to his wife announced a coming playfulness, and she laughed feebly—"no doubt Henry has had too much of greater interest to say; I must speak of the practical side of the question."

"Anne, dear, you mustn't think your father in any way disapproves of your choice. No; you have made us both very happy. Dear, dear Henry!"

Anne tried to speak, but could by no means steady her voice.

"You have, indeed, been fortunate in thus—at this early period of your life—securing the regard of a most worthy and excellent young man, and I rejoice to find you are sensible of this yourself. Still, you are both young. Henry's prospects—as he admits himself—are more satisfactory than are his present means; therefore it is my wish—as I have already explained to Henry, who concurs entirely in my reasons —that your marriage should not take place——"

"My marriage!" shrieked Anne, springing to her feet. "I'm not going to be married."

"Compose yourself, Anne; such agitation is unreasonable. Marriage is woman's natural vocation; without it she is incomplete, if not abnormal! But, as I just said, you are not to be married at present."

Anne had sat down again. "I beg your pardon, father, but there has been a complete misunderstanding. I refused Henry Stephens. Yes," she went on, in answer to a fragment from Mrs. Paton, audible on the ebb-tide of what the newspapers, with expressive vagueness, call a "sensation;"—"yes, Hester did see, but she has explained it wrong."

Whereupon, not too coherently, but still comprehensibly, she proceeded to explain it right. To herself, now that it was related, it sounded horribly silly; what is worse, the ambiguity of her position became even more glaringly apparent. It was rather to confirm than to confess her faith that she concluded, " He quite understood."

There was an awful pause; through it, Mrs. Paton's tears might be heard pattering on the newspaper upon her knee, like the drops that usher in a thunder-storm. It broke.

" I, however," said Captain Paton, beginning piano somewhere very low down in the bass, but gathering a fine crescendo as he proceeded, " I am far from understanding. But what I would give you to understand is that such—such—I may say such playing fast and loose with a young man whom you have conspicuously encouraged for weeks past, is not the conduct I expected from my daughter, or will tolerate in her. What, pray, has been the meaning of your behaviour towards him ever since your return?"

Anne was crying now, feeling, too, as simply naughty as ever she had done at eight.

"I'm not a young man," she sobbed, twisting her lovely shoulders. "Nobody has any right to ask a young woman, what are her intentions?"

In a war of words between a man and a woman, there usually comes a moment of signal defeat. Happy he who, in such a case, can fall back, simply and with dignity, on his authority, without fear of being disobeyed. That is what Captain Paton did.

After the brief but all-confessing silence which followed Anne's last remark, he announced that the discussion was unbecoming and unprofitable, bade Anne retire to her chamber and consider her ways, and wound up with a vague threat of renouncing her in case of disobedience, and a much more explicit reference to various far worthier young women who were at that moment earning, as governesses, the daily bread embittered by the supercilious sneers of their haughty employers. Mrs. Paton would have followed, but he sternly forbade it.

Anne went off crying, and, in her own room, she sat down and cried for a while still. Yet was she cheered, as only a woman can be, with the sense of having had the last word. She knew the victory was barren; but it is wonderful how many women will yield the substance of a dispute with a comparatively good grace, if the verbal victory be confessedly left with them. If men understood this better, they could oftener get their own way; it is because they will insist, not merely on being in the right—which ought to content any reasonable being—but on making their womankind acknowledge them to be in the right, that they fail.

Thus Anne was really in a more favourable frame of mind for reflection than she could ever have been had her father possessed a brighter genius for repartee. At first, of course, she vowed to herself that he might do his worst; never, never would she be the wife of Henry Stephens. This was heroic; but when she let her imagination raise the picture of what that worst might be, she began to wonder whether, in good truth, the game was worth the candle. She no longer shuddered at vague terrors; she did not shudder at the governess idea at all, but she shrugged her shoulders and slightly tip-tilted her nose. Few prospects could have been more distasteful. She cared little for the haughty employer, or for the spite and stings of the envious misses who would, of course, be her rivals; for these things she cared little, for she felt a not unjustifiable confidence of being able, under any circumstances, to give as good as she got. Nor was it the insolence of the equally haughty menials that she feared; for there never was a servant yet, in any establishment known to Anne, who was not her devoted follower and friend by the end of three days. What she recoiled from was, first, the children, next, the dulness—the solitude; not the loneliness, a fact of which she had no experience, but the mere withdrawal from the sight and intercourse of human beings. People she must have. To be surrounded, crowded, filled with the consciousness of humanity and of human interests; this, however vaguely, entered largely into her visions of an ideally enjoyable existence.

Thus reflecting, not on her ways, but on her prospects, she shook her head more vehemently; got to feel more and more, as the hours passed by, that strength of mind was an unpractical quality; that, her recent victory being taken into account, such odds would justify a carefully guarded surrender. She would capitulate, on no other condition than that of being allowed to march out with the honours of war; this much she thought she could extort.

Yes; she would capitulate. She sprang up, unagitated and decided, and went to the window to fling it wide open. She bent far out into the golden afternoon, if so she might catch a glimpse of that human world from which, for an age of four hours, she had been secluded. Four hours, in fact: but how many dreary weeks and months in foreshadowing! She was rewarded only by a glimpse of a baker's cart and a couple of girls on the side-walk, sentimentalizing over a toy-terrier one held in her arms; but, like the Ancient Mariner, she blessed them unawares. Yes: she would capitulate.

If any should consider such a conclusion weak and beneath the dignity of history (and Anne felt it weak herself), let them consider that those heroines of romance who defy, even unto fainting and semi-starvation, the fury of the grey tyrant father and the mysterious terrors of the eastern tower, had each and all one powerful sustaining motive. They had some one in the background—that being whom the melodramatist calls *Another;* and this makes all the difference. Anne had no one, not even an ideal ; and it is not easy to sacrifice one's self simply for a negative. It is true she did not want to marry. But then she did not know what she wanted instead. Not to be an old maid—a conventional figure in black bombazine and grey front ringlets, with flabby fingers and a shabby reticule bursting with tracts. Anne could not think of herself like that ; she was of a temperament to which death itself, though seldom enough thought of, would yet seem many times less unnatural and incomprehensible than old age. What did she want then ? Again and again had she tried to formulate her vague ideas ; but continually she failed. Each time she was brought back to a negative, which, by dint of repetition, began to seem unreasonable to herself.

She did not want to marry. Still, she had always supposed that some day or other she would have to do so. School-life, without awakening her heart, had enlightened her understanding on this point, or she thought it had. This being, then, her natural end, Henry, so far as she knew, was no worse than another; so far better, perhaps, that she had satisfactory experience of being able to manage him. The fact was that there was something Amazonian about Anne's moral organization; she was absolutely devoid of sentiment, as it is understood at her age. Flirtation she could understand, friendship she could understand; but to ordinary sentiment, to love of the quality that satisfactorily furnishes forth ninety-nine per cent. of young couples for their matrimonial voyage, to this no fibre of her being responded. It was at once a great deal too much, and infinitely too little. For the rest, of course, she was profoundly ignorant of what married life would practically be like. What girl is not? That it could, in any case, seriously interfere with her liberty was the last thing that occurred to her.

Once her mind was made up to an idea, Anne was not the girl to defer its execution. Still, there were difficulties in the way. But, for the first time that day, the fates were propitious to her. She was still debating how to let her parents know of her surrender, and yet guard her dignity and independence, when she heard a hall door open. It was the Stephens' and, flying again to the window, she saw Henry come down the path and turn in at their gate. In point of fact, he had forgotten his umbrella, and was come to fetch it.

The family were dressing for dinner; the servants, should they appear, were her sworn friends. Anne's resolution was taken. Silent as a bright shadow she slipped from the room, flew downstairs, and opened the door herself before Henry had time to ring.

There was a moment's awkwardness about the meeting, but Anne would do nothing to break it. She had had one look into Henry's face, and had got her cue. After one saucy flash on opening, she stood with eyes drooping and demure. She did not ask him what he had come for; she gave him no word of greeting— only waited.

"Dear Anne!" said Henry.

"Yes, Henry?"

"Surely we understand one another at

last. Not a word? Silence, they say gives consent. Ah, then, keep silence for ever!"

Anne's lips quivered, but she was silent.

"At least give me a sign."

The laughter had already died away; yet she neither wept, blushed, nor trembled. For a moment longer she stood, then all of a sudden she lifted her eyes to his. In them was a strange mixture of levity and seriousness; the eyes of the girl prophetic of the woman. She sighed a little, but smiled through it, a little shaking her head.

"I know you're not wise, Henry, and I suspect I'm not. But, since they wish it, and you will have it so"—with a sudden frank, almost boyish gesture, she put her hand into his—"there, it's a bargain!"

CHAPTER X.

"PEOPLE IN SOCIETY."

For the first few months of her engagement Anne was allowed to feel that virtue is its own reward. She had not looked forward to much active satisfaction from the step she had taken, therefore she was all the more agreeably surprised. For there was a sudden recognition of her independence, a relaxing of the discipline of pupilage, which was very pleasant. Then, on the first day on which he could conscientiously allow himself a holiday, Henry brought her a really handsome ring

—ruby and diamond, rather commonplace, but in good taste and effective—and Anne, who delighted in ornament, and who had but very, very little jewellery, was in ecstacies, and rejoiced over it to his heart's content.

She was really very well-behaved during his occasional visits, quite as much so as he required. For in a certain primitive fashion Anne was conscientious; when she had said it was a bargain she meant that it should be an honest one, honestly stood by. So far as her lights went, she meant to do her duty by Henry. The correspondence, which he expected to be frequent and regular, was a trial at first. But she used to take Hester into her confidence, under pretence of getting help with the spelling, and by judicious management would draw her on to compose the chief part of the letter. Hester, to whom all this was as thrilling as that first novel she had not yet read, was nothing loth, and Henry got many epistles which had little in them of Anne except the handwriting.

One of Anne's first steps was to try to conciliate Mrs. Stephens; but here, though she honestly did her best, exerting all her powers of adaptation, she was scarcely even partially successful. She put it all down to her future mother-in-law's objection to her personal character, and would come back from her daily visits despondent, wrathful, or perplexed, as the case might be.

"I think she hates me worse the more I try," she would complain to Hester. "I have tried everything, even to asking for a second helping of rice-pudding, and getting the receipt; but it is all no use. One day I offered to help the twins with their singing. They haven't such very bad voices; there's not much in them, but they don't distract you. Of course I put it more politely than that to her."

"Was she pleased?"

"You would have supposed she would be, wouldn't you? You know how she is always going on about *her* dear girls having had *so few* educational advantages as regards *fashionable accomplishments.* Well, she wasn't. She looked like—like—most like pickled thunder-cloud."

"Did she refuse?"

"I suppose she meant it for a refusal; but she made it into such a rigmarole about the misuse of talents, and the snares of the world, and the fate of the flatterer out of the 'Pilgrim's Progress,' that I scarcely know. She is so fond of quoting the 'Pilgrim's Progress'; but, if she meant that for me, she was out this time. I looked when I got home, and it was the pilgrims who came to grief, and not the flatterer at all. Nothing seems to have happened to him. It is my belief she scarcely ever does get the moral quite right; I mean always to look for the future. But what am I to do?"

"You mustn't get out of heart, dear; she is sure to come round at last. I'll go with you to-morrow if I can, and see if I can't keep things straight. Perhaps she is a little jealous over Henry; you see she has been accustomed to be first with him for so many years."

"She needn't be jealous of me, if that is all," said Anne, with candour. "Had I better tell her so? Shall I ask Henry not to give me more than an hour next time he comes? I don't mind," she added magnanimously.

"Oh no, dear!" said Hester, hastily. "That will only make matters worse. Take no notice; go on as you have been doing; you have been just sweet these last weeks."

Hester, indeed, was able to do a good deal towards keeping things straight, for Mrs. Stephens liked her as much as, ever since the night of the party, she had disliked Anne. Her first objections indeed had arisen from social ambition; but the personal objection had long since put that into the shade. Henry might have married Hester, and welcome. He might have married Cophetua's beggar-maid had he so pleased, for up to the date of her marriage that young lady is the most perfect instance on record of a silent woman. After her marriage *we* do not hear of her either. But Anne, in the first encounter, had proved herself anything but speechless or unready of speech, and, so far as she could hate, Mrs. Stephens hated her.

Anne's patience, never her strong point,

was failing at last, and a battle-royal seemed imminent, when, fortunately, an invitation came to both girls to spend a week or so in London. The invitation was from that very Lady Mary who had witnessed Anne's fancy-dress exhibition on the balcony at Richmond. She had taken one of her impulsive fancies to her on the spot, and made her daughter's acquaintance with the girls a pretext for carrying out her sudden whim.

The invitation did not tend to smooth matters between Anne and her mother-in-law elect. That her Mary's highest flights could but aspire to Hampstead, while Anne, certainly not her social superior, should be wafted, without effort, to the empyrean of Belgravia was galling enough. That Mary should not feel her wrongs was worse. When she found that the visit was to be made, she sent the girls a ceremonious invitation to the usual high tea, and proceeded to make things unpleasant for them. Even Hester could not win forgiveness, and Hester felt the particular form of aggravation much more than did Anne, for she had just the gentility instinct which Anne lacked. When Mrs. Stephens, by means of a judiciously worded message, called up Mary—hot, untidy, and rather smutty, covered with a kitchen apron, and faintly odorous of the coming toast—Anne jumped up, with unbecoming alacrity, from a genealogical disquisition on Lady Mary Ponsonby, and begged to be allowed to go and make toast too.

Poor Hester shrank, and wished herself fathoms underground, when Mrs. Stephens said, with a sigh chastened with a resigned smile—

"Indeed, my love, you mustn't think of

it. I couldn't conscientiously let *you* ruin *your* complexion."

"Oh, nothing hurts me!" said Anne, cheerfully. It was true enough to make Mrs. Stephens more irritable.

"Still, for you, there is no occasion even to run the risk. I make no apology for dear Mary; she is doing her duty. I wish, my dear, you would remove that smudge. A lady should try not to look like a kitchen-maid, even if she has to be one."

Mary obediently applied her apron to her cheek with a glance at Anne, which was returned with interest as regards expression and intelligence.

"Oh, Mary, Mary, you have put on your best gown already! What is to become of you when you are married, my poor child, I can't think! I suppose you fortunate young people"—smiling with playful cordiality at the Patons—"scarcely know what it is to have to think of such matters. Has that charming demi-toilette (is that the right name? I am so little in the way of hearing these things), that sweet gown your dear mother was choosing from those patterns the other day, has that been packed up yet, Anne? If not, it would be such a treat to Mary just to have a peep at it. People in society"—the tone here is simply indescribable—"have little idea at how small a cost to themselves they can give pleasure to their *less favoured* friends."

"If you don't think it would make dear Mary jealous," said Anne, sweetly.

"Are you afraid, my child?" said the mother searchingly, taking Mary's floury hand with anxious tenderness in her own.

"No, oh! no," exclaimed poor Mary, darting a look of pathetic remonstrance at

Anne. "I—I think I hear the cake—I mean the kettle—boiling over or something. Excuse me, dears," and she fled.

Anne felt herself very good for not going after her, but in pity to Hester she could but stay. At tea-time it was the same thing. Mrs. Stephens was apologetic over the muffins, and resigned over the raspberry jam. The wretched twins' lives were, for that hour, made a burden to them. Their dress, their manners, their silence and their speech, were not so much reprehended as compassionated, while the Paton girls were constantly appealed to as the inspired organs of the aristocracy. By the time they left the house, Hester was not far from tears; Anne relieved her feelings with a brief and uncomplimentary allusion to their hostess, then laughed and, almost as she did so, forgot all about it.

The next afternoon they were in London. They met with quite an enthusiastic reception. Lady Mary was nothing if not cordial; Louisa welcomed them with the same broad and genial smile with which she looked out upon the bright side of everything. She had never been "particular friends" of the Patons, that idea was entirely due to her mother, but she was general friends with all creation, and it with her. At dinner the girls met Mr. Ponsonby, of whom it is sufficient to say that he was gentlemanly, handsome, and intelligent, with a certain dignity of manner, partly acquired from the supposed necessity of making up for his wife's deficiencies in that respect.

Irish and impulsive, Lady Mary altogether was a good deal like her laugh; she was spontaneous. She found no difficulty in attaching herself with equal vehemence to characters and qualities the most dissimilar; and she was soon as much enchanted with Hester as if she had never been attracted by her exact antipodes. She was gushing, and marvellously devoid of tact; but she was quite genuine, and Hester, who liked expansiveness in the affections, returned her devotion. Anne, to whom she was no less effusive, remained almost unmoved. It is improbable that she was unsusceptible to flattery, but the key to that weakness of her nature had not yet been found; her heart did not open to Lady Mary's rather clumsy fumbling at that lock. The girl was not proud of her inherent Bohemianism; she saw nothing piquant or effective in it. She accepted it, as a condition of her being; it did not distress her, but she did not admire it. Lady Mary's skittish attempts at assuming the sentiments and deportment of a stage artist, (such as she conceived them,) though she knew it was done in her honour, merely moved her to good-natured contempt. She felt as she might have done if, to spare the feelings of a carroty guest, her hostess had come out in a red wig and waxed eloquent on the artistic merits of the shade. The affectation was kindly and well-intentioned, but it must be affectation, and, as such, she despised it. Socially and artistically, Bohemianism and red hair were still at a discount, and there was nothing prophetic in the soul of Anne.

Lady Mary was very happy in her two guests. Each was nearly perfect in her own style, and their styles were diametrically opposed. They kept her in a perpetual moral see-saw, and she enjoyed the sensation. Louisa made no effect anywhere; but the almost creative joy of a discoverer, which was hers when she brought out Anne in worldly society, scarcely surpassed the delights of showing off Hester at a Dorcas meeting, or taking her round the "district." For Lady Mary had a district, and from time to time would remember it in a rush of spasmodic energy. The house was always supplied with a certain number of half-covered tracts and half-made pinafores. For, when the outburst of remembrance came, she would clear off one lot and get half through another, which was thus only just in want of finishing off when the next spasm of recollection occurred. Hester was very happy in the work, and probably it was the suggestiveness of her very personality that made Lady Mary take up her parochial iron from the fire once more.

"It is just like the Wildgrave in the

poem, when the two huntsmen joined him," she said one day, with engaging frankness, to the girls themselves. "You recollect the lines—

> "'Who were those strangers, left and right,
>   Well may I guess but dare not tell;
> The right-hand steed was silver-white,
>   The left the swar—'

Ah! yes; dear me! something about the horse being in black and the rider too, wasn't it, Louisa? 'as well,' you know;" this with frantic signallings and palpable confusion.

Hester, whose acquaintance with the poets was strictly limited to L. E. L., and Mrs. Hemans, only wondered why Louisa went off into one of her fits of laughter. Anne tried to look as if she liked it, but with no marked success; and Henry Stephens, coming into the room at that moment, begged to be initiated into the joke. But no one gratified him.

Henry was on such terms with the family by this time that he could permit himself the inquiry. As soon as Lady Mary knew of Anne's engagement, she had insisted, in the kindness of her heart, on making Henry free of the house; and in his own discreet way he had availed himself of the freedom. Whether Anne had exactly counted on this turn of affairs, in anticipating the joys of London, may be doubted; but she had at least so much self-respect as to conceal her want of enthusiasm. Nevertheless, the first introduction to Henry sufficed to make the engagement a standing wonder to Lady Mary. She would have supposed it to be merely the result of a family compact, had not certain allusions of Anne's to her future mother-in-law seemed incompatible with such a solution. She tried to get some clue to the situation from Hester, but Hester did not even understand what it was she wanted to discover. Of course Anne loved him; she was going to be married to him, that must settle the question.

Lady Mary, who privately found Henry an insufferable bore, was less entirely satisfied. In truth, she had her own plan for her *protégée*—a notable one it was, nothing less than a match between Anne and the half-proscribed cousin, whom she had seen and made a note of in the balcony-scene which had been her first introduction to both. There was no particular reason why she should desire it; she knew nothing either of his means or of his character; but the idea of the *dénouement* struck her as romantic, and, as such, she would have liked to see it carried out, would have done her best to help carry it out, from a purely disinterested satisfaction in romance. Unfortunately she was far more romantic than was her rather unmanageable heroine. Anne showed so little interest in her cousin that Lady Mary gave up the attempt at moulding her mind and heart in despair. Even she could not persuade herself that the girl's indifference was anything but perfectly genuine. It seemed strange that Anne, caring so little, should remember so well; yet so it was.

That stolen visit to Uncle Will and Aunt Theresa had been the one adventure of a featureless childhood, and she remembered it with the vividness natural in such a case. But, except in comparatively rare moments of rebellion, it may be doubted whether it seemed as charming in recollection as it had done in fact. If it had been given to William Paton, in one of his happier moments, or even to

Aunt Theresa, to be the first figure to step into her life again out of the picture of the past, the effect produced might have been different. But it was George ; George to whom all her memories pointed as to something totally antagonistic to his surroundings. There was nothing in him which could idealize a memory, which her maturer understanding felt to require a good deal of idealization.

Of course Lady Mary knew all there was to be known, and perhaps some more, about the family history. Anne had never been reticent on the subject at school ; her actor uncle, and all his belongings and surroundings, had been the stock romance in real life of successive generations of her school-fellows; and Lady Mary had learned it all from Louisa. Of course the story had lost nothing by transmission, especially after the time that Anne got tired of telling it herself, and left it to be promulgated by whomsoever listed. By this time it was quite a fine study in myth-development. Coarse and unpleasant detail had disappeared; all the characters and circumstances were clothed with sentiment, and had assumed heroic proportions, and this just when, for Anne herself, the disillusion was becoming complete. She would have laughed, could she have guessed what the story had grown to; but she never even referred to it enough to have a chance of finding this out.

In one way, however, the fact that George had been the hero of her escapade, was a consolation. Had it been a stranger, the constant allusions to troubadours, serenades, Romeo and Juliet, and similar brilliantly novel comparisons, would have been intolerable. As it was, the evident absurdity amused till it began to weary her. All this about George! the very man, as she felt by instinct, who, even if there was not another woman in the world, would never think of her!

Finally, Lady Mary settled down to calling Anne, Blondel, and George, King Richard. She was always trying unsuccessfully to hum "O Richard! O mon roi!" in an allusive manner. Anne fervently congratulated herself on never having learned or met with the song; but she congratulated herself too early, for Lady Mary, finding her own attempts abortive, procured it for her, and the girl had to sing it whenever her hostess felt good-humouredly *maligne*.

Yet it was all done with such genuine unconsciousness of offence, that she could scarcely seriously resent it; and, in most ways, she was enjoying herself so thoroughly that such trifles could not noticeably detract from her happiness.. As for Lady Mary's dramatic intentions on her behalf, she never once suspected them. Nevertheless, that lady still vaguely cherished hopes and plans, having little suspicion, on her part, of the peculiar development of her romance which fate was preparing.

CHAPTER XI.

HESTER'S CONVERT.

ONE morning, when the girls' visit was fast drawing to a close, Hester got a letter which caused her considerable consternation. In it, Mrs. Paton informed them that mumps had broken out in the household. She herself was writing in bed, and Captain Paton, she grieved to say, was already showing symptoms impossible to mistake. She had written to Miss Robinson, at their old school, and she had kindly consented to receive them, and keep them till it should be safe for them to go back.

But Lady Mary scouted the idea of Miss Robinson. The girls must stay on with her; she sat down to write to that effect on the spot. Hester, to whom the letter of any law was very dear, had scruples, indeed; but eventually gave in, without much resistance. From that day, however, she began to droop. She was one of those people who cannot hear of a visit of the doctor to one of their friends without supposing it a prelude to that of the undertaker; between being unwell and being dangerously ill she saw little or no difference.

Lady Mary was distressed, and as, by this time, Anne was well launched upon the world, and could get chaperons for the asking, she devoted herself more to Hester. The very next afternoon, seeing that the girl had been fretting quietly all day at not getting another letter, she offered the distraction which seemed to suit her visitor's taste the best—a visit to the district.

Hester accepted with some approach to alacrity, and they set out accordingly. They left Anne, all bedecked and radiant, waiting to be called for by one of her now numerous fashionable acquaintances. She was in her best gown, and her highest spirits; Hester, slightly shabby and subdued. The contrast was striking, but it was Lady Mary alone who felt like Cinderella, and, absurd though it seems, she really did look down at her old mantle with a sort of pang. She was too good-natured actually to repent the sacrifice; but she was absent and abstracted for some time, and her disjointed conversation betrayed a lingering of heart among the giddy haunts of pleasure. She did not quite recover till they were within a few streets of their destination.

It must not be supposed that Lady Mary's district was of the lowest type.

The region which enjoyed her spasmodic benevolence was one of small public-houses, and still smaller indefinite shops. Here and there, between the display of winkles and superannuated apples, a yellow spotted card, in a dingy window, announced a mantua-maker or a chimney-sweep, an undertaker or a monthly nurse.

It was moderately respectable, and not at all exciting; but Hester, who had no craving for sensation, was well satisfied with it.

Still, respectable though the neighbourhood was, she had never yet ventured a step in it out of Lady Mary's sight, and it was with some dismay that, on this afternoon, she found herself obliged to do so. They were about to visit an old pensioner on an upper story when, at the very door of his room, Lady Mary suddenly remembered that she had promised to bring him a packet of his greatest remaining consolation — snuff, and had completely forgotten all about it.

"Will you go, my dear, and just get me two pennyworth, and bring it up, while I go up to Mrs. Wilkins? I wouldn't ask you, only I really cannot get up all these dreadful stairs again, and he will be so disappointed."

"But," faltered Hester, "I can't go and ask for snuff."

"Oh! at any of the shops," said Lady Mary vaguely, rummaging in her bag for an Infirmary ticket for Mrs. Wilkins; "you know things are so mixed together in those little places, I have even seen oranges and dried herrings side by side. Dear, dear, where can the thing have got to?" She was working her way up the stairs as she spoke, and the last Hester heard of her was a triumphant: "Ah! here; I thought I couldn't have forgotten *that.*" Then a door above opened, and she was left alone with her commission. The very strongest instinct in her nature was obedience, passive and unquestioning, and now, with inward trembling, she descended to the street.

She passed several shops, with the excuse to herself that it could be no use asking there; at last she fixed on one differing in no respect from the others, simply because she had gone further than she meant and felt frightened. Ill-luck usually pursues the timid, and it pursued Hester. The shop of her selection was served by a hobble-de-hoy, at the age when veneration is smallest and the love of tormenting strongest. Business being slack, a like-minded friend had dropped in to keep him company, and was lounging against the counter, looking into the street. Hester came on with that air of uncertainty as to her intentions which irresistibly attracts notice. At the window she paused, and contemplated the contents with the feeblest pretence of making up her mind, then desperately entered.

"I want... Do you keep snuff?" she asked in a sort of gasp.

The youth addressed winked at his friend, who casually took up a position at the door.

"Sorry to say we don't, miss—leastways, not the quality as you're accustomed to," he said facetiously.

"Oh!" said Hester hastily, too desperately eager to get it, and go, to realize what she was saying, "I dare say what you have will be quite good enough; it isn't for myself I want it."

The friend at the door burst into a roar of exquisite mirth, which convulsed his whole figure.

"Hold your noise, Willum," said his comrade severely. "Never mind him, miss."

"Will you be so kind as to let me have it at once?" said Hester, the tears already in her voice. "I am in a hurry."

"Oh! didn't I say we hadn't got any? Well, now, how forgetful of me."

"Could you tell me where to get some?"

"Certainly, miss. Take the first to the left beyond the third right-hand lamp-post, then the second to the right, and the first to the right again, and the third but one to the left, and there you are."

"Oh! thank you," said the victim, as fully and evidently bewildered as he could have hoped; "I'm sorry to have given you so much trouble."

"Nothing else we can show you to-day? Oranges? nuts? gingerbread?" thrusting each article before her with lightning-like rapidity. " Here ; these conwersation tablets : ' Do you love me ? ' ' Ask papa ! ' Ah ! " smacking his lips as he consumed the suggestive dainty with a strong odour of peppermint, " don't I wish I could ! "

Another outburst of hilarity from the doorway.

" How dare you ! " cried Hester. " You, sir, let me out."

For William was so posted in the narrow doorway as to render egress impossible.

" Must pay toll first," he said ; and with an expressive labial pantomime conveyed to her the nature of the required tribute. Hester, her eyes wide with horror, turned for protection to the other, but he was gazing abstractedly at the ceiling. And then William put a hand on her shoulder. Hester screamed.

Almost simultaneously with the scream, the astonished youth felt himself seized by the collar, violently shaken, and hurled some way into the street. There he fell, and lay for some seconds more mentally than physically stunned. When he recovered he deemed it advisable to walk in another direction.

Inside the shop, his assailant turned sharply to the accomplice.

"Go and get the lady a glass of water, and be quick about it, if you don't want the best thrashing you ever had in your life."

Then, as the boy disappeared, he turned to Hester who was crying helplessly with choking, half-suppressed sobs. He drew an old box out of a heap of odds and ends and gently made her sit down. He showed no discomposure at the sight of her tears, and said nothing to try to check them. In fact, he did not speak at all till his messenger came back with the water; then, in a voice which Hester recognized as the voice of authority, he said : "Now drink some of this."

She obeyed, with an instantaneousness which seemed to please him, for he smiled.

"Now you must rest here for five minutes, then you shall tell me where I am to take you to. No, never mind thanking me; don't try to talk yet at all."

Something in his manner checked her tears as much as, or more than, the water had done. Before two of the five minutes were up she had dried her eyes; then she looked up at him, in obedient silence, with a tremulous but eloquent smile. The surroundings were the reverse of romantic, yet the hero of the scene, at least, looked fit for a hero of romance—or so Hester thought, as she half furtively contemplated the tall figure standing above her, the chestnut hair with eyes to match—eyes which took but little light from the smile which was relaxing the rather stern lines of the mouth; features almost ideally correct, and the bearing and gesture of a ruler by divine right. Presently he said:

"And now where am I to take you? Surely you have not come to this part alone?"

Hester explained, but could not refrain from defending the character of the district.

"I know everybody there; none of our people would behave so. Indeed you mustn't think it. This part does not belong to Lady Mary."

Then she turned to the shop-boy, who had been a sufficiently subdued third in the scene.

"I believe your friend William was thrown—fell down just now. I should be sorry to think he had been hurt on my account, and you may tell him so. I suppose neither of you quite understood how much you were annoying me; but I hope you will act differently for the future. I believe you are in Mr. Clarke's parish; there is a very excellent class for young men at his house on Thursday evenings, which I hope you will attend, and take your friend too. I will try to find out who your visitor is, and ask her to speak to you about it. Good afternoon."

It was all said with such gentle condescension, the feeling of being on her own ground gave such an air of spiritual authority to her tone and manner, that her champion looked at her with wonder, half venerating, half amused.

"I hope he *will* go," she said anxiously, as soon as they were in the street. "I have a little leaflet here which would have been just the thing for him, but I never like to give things in other people's districts; it so often makes unpleasantness and misunderstandings. There was almost a quarrel over something of the kind, at the last visitors' meeting."

"Professional jealousy is a great trial to the single-minded in any calling," he said, with becoming gravity; "but it is a thing that has to be counted on."

"It seems hard to call it jealousy," sighed Hester; "but I suppose it must really be something of the kind. You speak as if you understood about it, too. Do you work much in this part?"

"I have never been here before to-day."

"Oh! I thought, perhaps—— You

aren't the new Scripture-reader?" she asked shyly.

He stopped short. The look of amusement that had flashed for a moment across his face faded, and was succeeded by one almost of pain.

"I cannot allow you to think so much better of me than I deserve," he said. "My experience was learned in a very different school. I came here to-day simply on a matter of most worldly business. One of our scene-shifters lives in the next street; he has absented himself without explanation for two nights past, and I was sent to look him up."

"One of those men that change the scenes at—a theatre?" said Hester, the soft light dying out of her face.

"At the theatre, with which I am connected. Yes."

She walked on in silence.

"Now I have shocked you," he said rather savagely.

"No; I'm not shocked. But I am sorry—I am *very* sorry," she added, after a pause. "But very likely you have never thought."

"Perhaps not. Is not that your friend's carriage? No, thank you; you will be quite safe now, and I would rather not come on."

"Are you angry with me?" said Hester, rather wistfully. "I ought to have had nothing for you but thanks."

"No, not with *you*," he said. "You spoke as you thought right."

"And—don't be annoyed with me, now —you *will* think? Will you let me give you this?"

Shyly, and with rosy blushes, she drew out of her reticule a little tract. She scarcely dared to offer it; but he put out his hand, and took it from her.

"Thank you," he said gravely; "I shall not forget."

He bowed, and left her, turning back along the street. In another minute Lady Mary was listening with delighted excitement, to Hester's account of her adventures. But when she would have extracted a full and particular description of the deliverer, she found the girl vague, and rather short in her answers.

Meanwhile, George Paton was walking slowly down the street, a sort of smile on his lips, and a good deal of bitterness in his heart. By-and-by, he gave a look at the leaflet he still held loosely in his hand. It was entitled: "What are you to-night?" and seemed to be addressed to the profession. But he did not read it then; to tell the truth, though he kept it for long, he never did read it at all.

As a dissuasive, he certainly did not

need it; never had needed it. It was no prickings of conscience on that score that made him thrust it out of sight, with an exclamation of impatience. He had disclaimed, and perhaps at the time truly, any vexation with Hester. But the whole incident had annoyed him exceedingly, and now, as he recalled it, she came in for a share in his annoyance. But this was so manifestly unjust that a reaction soon set in. For how could she have known? And really she had been very brave about delivering her testimony, according to her lights; it had not been done without an effort. Considering her unmistakeable conviction that every member of his profession must needs be a hopeless reprobate, she had, indeed, spoken with much forbearance and moderation. Of course he was aware that he was no more a reprobate than he was a Scripture-reader. But he could repel the flattery, whereas a repudiation of that tacit assumption of guilt would have lacked both force and grace. The result was, no doubt, an unfortunate misunderstanding; but he was accustomed to mortifications arising from the nature of his calling, there was no reason why he should take any special notice of this one. And yet he did. He began to feel thoroughly out of humour with himself. Many men in his place would have blamed circumstances, but that was a satisfaction George did not allow himself, though he would have had considerable justification for doing so.

He thought he would relieve his feelings by giving a bit of his mind to Hester's persecutor; an expression of opinion very different to that with which she herself had favoured the offender. He recalled that speech with some amusement: how child-like she was in her womanliness, how quaint in her demureness; yet beyond a doubt she was as unaffected as she was quaint, and as good as she was pretty.

When he got to the shop the boy greeted him with irreproachable civility—his tribute to that physical superiority which, alone, he valued or recognized.

"You have come for the young lady's purse, sir?" he said. "I found it on the counter just after she left."

George took the purse, but was not to be thus dissuaded from delivering his lecture, which he did with sufficient affectation of bluster to impress his auditor considerably. Perhaps he really felt happier after this, at least it was with some appearance of interest that he proceeded to examine the purse for a clue to its owner's address.

The purse happened to be Lady Mary's,

and one or two of her cards were in an
out-of-the-way compartment. It was too
late for him to return it that night, he had
to hurry back to be in time for the performance ; but he looked forward with a certain
pleasure to restoring it on the morrow.

The first person he met as he was making
his way to the dressing-room, on his return,
was that popular favourite, Miss Florrie
Mortimer. She was to appear that night
in a new part, which meant a new dress :
both part and dress were, to say the least,
dashing, and both exactly suited her ;
consequently she was in the highest spirits.
She greeted George with some familiar
chaff; he thought it exceptionally vulgar,
even for Florrie. As he was taking off
his coat, a paper fell out of one of his
pockets ; picking it up hastily, he just
caught sight of the heading as he thrust it
back : " What are you to-night ? "

What was he? He did not hesitate for epithets: trifler, buffoon, mountebank, these were the best titles he allowed himself, and he had so applied them often enough before. "What are you to-night?" The old bitterness of impotent degradation, old yet ever new, came over him with tenfold force; but, with it, this time, something which might be the germ of a resolution.

The next afternoon, Anne, coming back towards dusk from one of her innumerable engagements, saw two extra hats in the hall. One was Henry's, and like him; the other was strange to her. A rapid questioning of the footman resulted in a discovery which set her whole being dancing with delight; there was a conjunction to be seen above which promised sport of a kind she could thoroughly appreciate.

She was ready in about two minutes,

and reached the drawing-room door just as the servant was going in with the tea-tray. She came in softly behind him, and stood for a moment in the doorway to look.

Lady Mary was beaming; this Anne had foreseen. Hester was looking shy, but pleased, and Henry interested, with the aggravating interest which a philosophical philanthropist may feel in a converted bargee. George, it was clear, had taken the measure of him and his interest, but seemed to have found some attraction strong enough to overcome his repulsion in that direction.

Anne stood where she was, and, very gently, allowed herself to laugh. Silvery-sweet as her laugh was, there was always a curious ring about it; it was rather the laughter of a sprite than of a mortal. George and Henry both looked round. Henry, with a touch of pride, turned his eyes, half unconsciously, towards the other man, for in sooth the girl was a dazzling vision. But George looked more puzzled than anything else; some memory was haunting him. All at once it took shape; Lady Mary saw it flash into his eyes, and, most unreasonably, rejoiced. He had it now: a memory of a suburban road on an afternoon in spring, a sunny afternoon, sweet with lilac and hawthorn blooms; of a voice ringing from the prim-looking house; then, standing transfixed on the balcony, a dainty figure in doublet and hose, the betraying gold already rolling in waves from under the white-plumed cap. A sort of smile passed over his face, comparable, for frigidity, to a gleam of sun on an iceberg. Anne saw it, and knew that her secret was known, knew also that, if only from sheer indifference, he would not betray it, and she was rather glad.

Lady Mary caught it too, and warmed it from the glow of her own imagination.

"I think, Mr. Paton," she said delightedly, "I need not introduce this cousin; she has often told me how you met before."

Anne did not trouble to refute this astounding statement. She smiled sweetly and gave him her hand.

"I have not forgotten how kind you were to me," she said, "and I think you must have been Hester's champion yesterday."

Hester nodded, with pleased eyes.

"She is very unlucky," Anne went on; "and she doesn't care for adventures, like I do."

Lady Mary giggled ecstatically, and tried to catch the visitor's eye. Anne thought it time to change the subject.

"Uncle Will is still on the stage, I know," she said. "Does Aunt Theresa act still?"

"Not often. I do not think she ought

to do it at all. The excitement and fatigue are too great for her now; she suffers for it afterwards."

"Do you find it wildly exciting?" asked Anne.

"Nearly as exciting as the treadmill, and quite as enjoyable."

"I can understand that," said Henry, benevolently. "Yet I would not have you suppose that I am of those who have an absolute and uncompromising prejudice against the stage. On the contrary, I conceive that it may be the vehicle of much moral instruction; slightly to parody the words of the poet, 'a *play* may catch him who a sermon flies.' It is a great pleasure to me to have this opportunity of gathering the opinion of one who has had such exceptional opportunities of studying the question. What is your estimate of the stage as an educative force?"

"So far as the audience is concerned the idea is a complete fallacy; what its educational value is to the actors themselves— I scarcely care to enter upon that subject here."

"Dear me, I am sorry to hear this; very sorry. May I not hope you are prejudiced? Surely, to commune as it were in the intimacy of daily life with the spirit of the immortal Shakespeare——"

"We don't," said George, drily; "not if we can help it."

"Indeed? You surprise me!" He brightened considerably, nevertheless. "But that accounts for it; no doubt that accounts for it."

Here a peculiar smile on George's face, boding no good, induced Henry to leave off with this decorous semblance of victory. He had been secretly trying to win Anne's admiration by this exhibition of large-mindedness; and it was trying to have been large-minded for nothing, after all. For her part she understood enough to be willing to be gracious.

"I have learned the accompaniment to that song of yours, Henry," she said, by way of a reward. "Shall I play it for you?"

The piano was in the further room, an arrangement which worked well at small musical entertainments, as neither talkers nor performers interfered with each other. Henry went off willingly. He possessed a good uninteresting baritone voice, of ordinary drawing-room power. There was nothing in it to hold the attention, and, after the first moment of complimentary silence, Hester had no scruple in resuming the conversation, only slightly lowering her always soft low voice.

Generally speaking, Hester was a shy

girl; but two things that day set her at ease. She saw in George at once a possible convert, and a relation; towards the convert shyness would, in any case, have been swallowed up in zeal, towards the relation it could not exist. The idea of the family, even to the thirteenth collateral, was as strong in Hester as in any Scotchman, and implied, through all its degrees of distance, a share in the safe and familiar liberties of home. She was glad George was her cousin; she was neither more nor less glad of it because she had first been interested in him as her deliverer. The claim of blood spoke louder than the claim of personal gratitude.

"It must be dreadful having to go on day after day doing a thing you hate," she said sympathetically.

George laughed, not very cheerfully.

"Oh, you must not take it tragically.

It is all in the day's work; and we are a gay, light-hearted set. Every one says so."

Hester gently shook her pretty brown head.

"I would rather hear you say you hate it," she said, with the manner she would have used to an erring and defiant Sunday-school boy. "I can see that the life does not really make you happy."

"How should it? To lie down, night by night, with the agreeable consciousness that you have been spending some hours in making a conspicuous fool of yourself; to pass your days killing time as best you may, till the time comes round for making a fool of yourself again."

Hester was a little shocked at the strength of his expressions, but reflected that his conversion was but new, and refrained from rebuke.

"I am very sorry for you," she said,

gently, "and yet I cannot help being glad to see that it disgusts you. Anything must be better than not even to feel the degradation."

Often as George had used that identical word himself, he did not altogether enjoy hearing it from her.

"You are rather severe," he said.

"I did not mean to be," faltered Hester. But already George had changed his mind.

"You ought to have meant it, then. What can it be but degradation? To be so habitually and deliberately unreal that unreality becomes a second nature, and it is natural to be affected. To outrage self-respect, by flaunting before the world a counterfeit mockery of every sentiment and situation which a man should seal up in most sacred reticence. An actor may have nothing sacred; for him everything has been rehearsed and publicly exhibited;

everything, even up to love and death. And the object of his simulated passion may be a scorn and horror to him behind the scenes; while the dying parent cracks a whispered joke, between his gasps, to the son who kneels to receive his blessing. A degradation!"

"But then," said Hester, pleasantly impressed by his vehemence and absolutely uncomprehending his words, "seeing it all so well, and feeling it so strongly, why should you not break away from it all? Oh, do!" she went on, with increasing animation as she seemed to see him hesitate. "I'm sure papa would help you in any way he could; he would do so in any case, because you are his nephew; and when he knows all you did for me——"

Here George fairly laughed.

"Well, you did; it was no laughing matter to me, and never will be," she said, with gentle warmth. "Won't you write to papa, and tell him how you want to get free of all this sad unsatisfactory life? Just put it before him, will you?"

Even if his own mind had been made up on the subject, he could not have been ready with an affirmative answer at such short notice. But he was spared the awkwardness of a refusal, for just then the music ceased; an instinctive move and murmur of thanks made an excuse for breaking off a dialogue which was becoming embarrassing, and a few minutes later he took his leave.

There was a moment's pause after he was gone. With him, Lady Mary, with a slight interior sigh, was dismissing the shadow of a coming romance.

"Shall I sing 'Oh, Richard!'?" said Anne, amiably.

Some vague suspicion of what Lady

Mary's expectations had been had dawned upon her.

"No, child," said her hostess, and the sigh came to the surface. "I won't be selfish about it, and I am sure you are quite tired of it. Sing something else."

END OF VOL. I.

www.ingramcontent.com/pod-product-compliance
Lightning Source LLC
Chambersburg PA
CBHW022104230426
43672CB00008B/1280